THE
VAGINA
MONOLOGUES

THE VAGINA MONOLOGUES

The V-Day Edition

Eve Ensler

VILLARD

NEW YORK

VILLARD BOOKS is a registered trademark of Random House, Inc.
Colophon is a trademark of Random House, Inc.

An earlier edition of this work was published in 1998
by Villard Books, a division of Random House, Inc.

Originally produced by HOME for Contemporary Theatre and Art
at HERE, Randy Rollison, artistic director, and Barbara Busackino,
producing director, in association with Wendy Evans Joseph.
Produced Off-Broadway by David Stone, Willa Shalit, Nina
Essman, Dan Markley/Mike Skipper, and the Araca Group.

Library of Congress Cataloging-in-Publication Data

Ensler, Eve.
The vagina monologues / Eve Ensler.—Rev. ed.
p.   cm.
ISBN 0-375-50565-2—ISBN 0-375-75698-1 (tradepaper)
1. Monologues.   2. Vagina.   3. Women.
PS3555.N75V3   2001
812'.54—dc21   00-043844

Villard Books website address: www.villard.com
Printed in the United States of America on acid-free paper

4 6 8 9 7 5 3

Revised Edition

Book design by Caroline Cunningham

For Ariel, who rocks my vagina

and explodes my heart

I come from the "down there" generation. That is, those were the words—spoken rarely and in a hushed voice—that the women in my family used to refer to all female genitalia, internal or external.

It wasn't that they were ignorant of terms like *vagina, labia, vulva,* or *clitoris.* On the contrary, they were trained to be teachers and probably had more access to information than most.

It wasn't even that they were unliberated, or "straitlaced," as they would have put it. One grandmother earned money from her strict Protestant church by ghostwriting sermons—of which she didn't believe a word—and then earned more by betting it on horse races. The other was a suffragist, educator, and even an early political candidate, all to the alarm of many in her Jewish community. As for my own mother, she had been a pioneer newspaper reporter years before I was born, and continued to take pride in bringing up her two daughters in a more enlightened way than she had been raised. I don't remember her using any of the slang words that made the female body seem dirty or shameful, and I'm grateful for that. As you'll see in these pages, many daughters grew up with a greater burden.

Nonetheless, I didn't hear words that were accurate, much less prideful. For example, I never once heard the word *clitoris.* It would be years before I learned that females possessed the only organ in the human body with no function other than to feel pleasure. (If such an organ were unique to the male body, can you imagine how much we would hear about it—and what it would be used to justify?) Thus, whether I was learning to talk, to spell, or to take care of my own body, I was told the name of each of its amazing parts—except in one unmentionable area. This left me unprotected against the shaming words and dirty jokes of the school yard and, later, against the popular belief that men, whether as lovers or physicians, knew more about women's bodies than women did.

I first glimpsed the spirit of self-knowledge and freedom that you will find in these pages when I lived in India for a couple of years after college. In Hindu temples and shrines I saw the lingam, an abstract male genital symbol, but I also saw the yoni, a female genital symbol, for the first time: a flowerlike shape, triangle, or double-pointed oval. I was told that thousands of years ago, this symbol had been worshiped as more powerful than its male counterpart, a belief that carried over into Tantrism, whose central tenet is man's inability to reach spiritual fulfillment except through sexual and emotional union with woman's superior spiritual energy. It was a belief so deep and wide that even some of the woman-excluding, monotheistic religions that came later retained it in their traditions, although such beliefs were (and still are) marginalized or denied as heresies by mainstream religious leaders.

For example: Gnostic Christians worshiped Sophia as the female Holy Spirit and considered Mary Magdalene the wisest of Christ's disciples; Tantric Buddhism still teaches that Buddhahood resides in the vulva; the Sufi mystics of Islam believe that *fana,* or rapture, can be reached only through Fravashi, the female spirit; the Shekina of Jewish mysticism is a version of Shakti, the female soul of God; and even the Catholic church included forms of Mary worship that focused more on the Mother than on the Son. In many countries of Asia, Africa, and other parts of the world where gods are still depicted in female as well as in male forms, altars feature the Jewel in the Lotus and other representations of the lingam-in-the-yoni. In India, the Hindu goddesses Durga and Kali are embodiments of the yoni powers of birth and death, creation and destruction.

Still, India and yoni worship seemed a long way from American attitudes about women's bodies when I came home. Even the sexual revolution of the 1960s only made more women sexually available to more men. The "no" of the 1950s was just replaced with a constant, eager "yes." It was not until the feminist activism of the 1970s that there began to be alternatives to everything from patriarchal religions to Freud (the distance from A to B), from the double standard of sexual behavior to the single standard of patriarchal/political/religious control over women's bodies as the means of reproduction.

Those early years of discovery are symbolized for me by such sense memories as walking through Judy Chicago's *Woman House* in Los Angeles, where each room was created by a different woman artist, and where I discovered female symbolism in my own culture for the first time. (For example, the shape we call a heart—whose symmetry resembles the vulva far more than the asymmetry of the organ that shares its name—is probably a residual female genital symbol. It was reduced from power to romance by centuries of male dominance.) Or sitting in a New York coffee shop with Betty Dodson (you will meet her in these pages), trying to act cool while she electrified eavesdroppers with her cheerful explanation of masturbation as a liberating force. Or coming back to *Ms.* magazine to find, among the always humorous signs on its bulletin board: IT'S 10 O'CLOCK AT NIGHT—DO YOU KNOW WHERE YOUR CLITORIS IS? By the time feminists were putting CUNT POWER! on buttons and T-shirts as a way of reclaiming that devalued word, I could recognize the restoration of an ancient power. After all, the Indo-European word *cunt* was derived from the goddess Kali's title of Kunda or Cunti, and shares the same root as *kin* and *country.*

These last three decades of feminism were also marked by a deep anger as the truth of violence against the female body was revealed, whether it took the form of rape, childhood sexual abuse, anti-lesbian violence, physical abuse of women, sexual harassment, terrorism against reproductive freedom, or the international crime of female genital mutilation. Women's sanity was saved by bringing these hidden experiences into the open, naming them, and turning our rage into positive action to reduce and heal violence. Part of the tidal wave of creativity that has resulted from this energy of truth telling is this play and book.

When I first went to see Eve Ensler perform the intimate narratives in these pages—gathered from more than two hundred interviews and then turned into poetry for the theater—I thought: *I already know this: it's the journey of truth telling we've been on for the past three decades.* And it is. Women have entrusted her with their most intimate experiences, from sex to birthing, from the undeclared war against women to the new freedom of love between women. On every page, there is the power of saying the unsayable—as there is in the behind-the-scenes story of the book itself. One publisher paid an advance for it, then, on sober second thought, allowed Eve Ensler to keep the money if she would take the book and its v-word elsewhere. (Thank Villard for publishing all of women's words—even in the title.)

But the value of *The Vagina Monologues* goes beyond purging a past full of negative attitudes. It offers a personal, grounded-in-the-body way of moving toward the future. I think readers, men as well as women, may emerge from these pages not only feeling more free within themselves—and about each other—but with alternatives to the old patriarchal dualism of feminine/masculine, body/ mind, and sexual/spiritual that is rooted in the division of our physical selves into "the part we talk about" and "the part we don't."

If a book with *vagina* in the title still seems a long way from such questions of philosophy and politics, I offer one more of my belated discoveries.

In the 1970s, while researching in the Library of Congress, I found an obscure history of religious architecture that assumed a fact as if it were common knowledge: the traditional design of most patriarchal buildings of worship imitates the female body. Thus, there is an outer and inner entrance, labia majora and labia minora; a central vaginal aisle toward the altar; two curved ovarian structures on either side; and then in the sacred center, the altar or womb, where the miracle takes place—where males give birth.

Though this comparison was new to me, it struck home like a rock down a well. *Of course,* I thought. *The central ceremony of patriarchal religions is one in which men take over the yoni-power of creation by giving birth symbolically. No wonder male religious leaders so often say that humans were born in sin— because we were born to female creatures. Only by obeying the rules of the patriarchy can we be reborn through men. No wonder priests and ministers in skirts sprinkle imitation birth fluid over our heads, give us new names, and promise rebirth into everlasting life. No wonder the*

*male priesthood tries to keep women away from the altar,
just as women are kept away from control of our own
powers of reproduction. Symbolic or real, it's all devoted
to controlling the power that resides in the female body.*

Since then, I've never felt the same estrange-
ment when entering a patriarchal religious struc-
ture. Instead, I walk down the vaginal aisle,
plotting to take back the altar with priests—
female as well as male—who would not disparage
female sexuality, to universalize the male-only
myths of Creation, to multiply spiritual words
and symbols, and to restore the spirit of God in all
living things.

If overthrowing some five thousand years of
patriarchy seems like a big order, just focus on cel-
ebrating each self-respecting step along the way.

I thought of this while watching little girls
drawing hearts in their notebooks, even dotting
their *i*'s with hearts, and I wondered: *Were they
magnetized by this primordial shape because it was so
like their own bodies?* I thought of it again while listening to a group of twenty or so diverse nine- to

sixteen-year-old girls as they decided to come up with a collective word that included everything— vagina, labia, clitoris. After much discussion, "power bundle" was their favorite. More important, the discussion was carried on with shouts and laughter. I thought: *What a long and blessed way from a hushed "down there."*

I wish my own foremothers had known their bodies were sacred. With the help of outrageous voices and honest words like those in this book, I believe the grandmothers, mothers, and daughters of the future will heal their selves—and mend the world.

CONTENTS

INTRODUCTION

I am not sure why I was chosen. I didn't, for example, have girlhood fantasies about becoming "vagina lady" (which I am often called, sometimes loudly across a crowded shoe store). I could not have imagined that I would one day be talking about vaginas on talk shows in places like Athens, Greece, chanting the word *vagina* with four thousand wild women in Baltimore, or having thirty-two public orgasms a night. These things were not in my plans. In this sense, I don't think I had much to do with *The Vagina Monologues.* It possessed me.

I see now that I was a prime candidate. I was a playwright. I had for years written plays based on interviews with people. I was a feminist. I had been violated sexually and physically by my father. I had exhibitionist tendencies. I have been known to outrage, and I longed with all of my being to find a way back into my vagina.

I don't really remember how it began: a conversation with an older woman about her vagina; her saying contemptuous things about her genitals that shocked me and got me thinking about what other women thought about their vaginas. I remember asking friends, who surprised me with their openness and willingness to talk. There was one friend in particular who told me that if her vagina got dressed, it would wear a beret. She was going through a French phase.

I definitely do not remember writing the piece. Simply put, I was taken—used by the

Vagina Queens. I never outlined the play or consciously shaped it. As a matter of fact, the whole process was totally off the record. I interviewed women about their vaginas while I was writing my "real" play. It was my partner, Ariel Orr Jordan (who, I am now convinced, was somehow on the payroll of the Vagina Queens), who got me to take it seriously and helped me conceive the piece and make a plan. But even then, to some degree, *The Vagina Monologues* has never really been any of my business.

I show up. I exercise to stay in shape. I drink plenty of power mocha frappuccinos. I try to stay out of the way. Here, for example, are some of the mysteries:

I was never a performer. It did not occur to me that I was actually performing *The Vagina Monologues* until I had been doing it for about three years. Before this point, I felt merely as if I were telling very personal stories that had been generously told to me. I felt strangely, and at times fiercely, protective of these women and their stories. I could not move when I was telling the stories. I had to remain seated in a high-back stool, with a place to rest my feet. It was like climbing into a spaceship every night. I had to speak into a microphone, even in places where I could easily be heard. The microphone functioned as a kind of steering wheel at times, an accelerator at others.

For the first years, I needed to wear stockings and heavy boy shoes to perform the piece. Then later, once my director, Joe Mantello, got me to take off my shoes, I could only do it barefoot.

I had to hold 5-by-8 cards in my hands all through the performance every night, even though I had the piece memorized. It was as if the women I had interviewed were made present by those cards, and I needed them there with me.

Vagina stories found me, as did the people who wanted to produce the play or bring it to their town. Whenever I have tried to write a monologue to serve a politically correct agenda, for example, it always fails. Note the lack of monologues about menopause or transgendered women. I tried. *The Vagina Monologues* is about attraction, not promotion.

Many things that have happened in the life of *The Vagina Monologues* seem completely surreal and at the same time completely logical. Here are examples:

Newspaper Headlines:

THAT GIRL GOES DOWN THERE (Marlo Thomas in *TVM*)

MAYOR'S WIFE TALKS DIRTY (Donna Hanover's decision to be in *TVM*)

Red boas on the front page of six London papers the day after V-Day at the Old Vic—newsstands in Britain look like the vagina sea.

TV:

Kathie Lee Gifford chants the word *vagina* with Calista Flockhart and her studio audience on *Live with Regis and Kathie Lee.*

David Letterman tries to say *vagina,* but can't.

Barbara Walters confesses on *The View* that

she was embarrassed by *TVM* and thought it was strident. She later recants.

CNN does a ten-minute special on *TVM* and never mentions the word.

Dharma's and Greg's parents are buying tickets to *TVM* on an episode.

Vagina Occurrences:

Glenn Close gets 2,500 people to stand and chant the word *cunt*.

Tovah Feldmanstern was denied the right to direct *TVM* at her all-girls progressive high school, so she directs it independently.

A woman rabbi sends me a hamantasch and describes its vaginal meanings.

There is now a Cunt Workshop at Wesleyan University.

A woman brings her uterus to the theater to have me sign it.

A young man makes and serves me a vagina salad for dinner with his parents in Atlanta, Georgia. Bean sprouts are pubic hair.

Roseanne performs "What Does Your Vagina Smell Like?" in her underwear for two thousand people. She makes up her own lines, one of them being: "What does your vagina smell like?" ANSWER: "My husband's face."

Alanis Morissette and Audra McDonald sing the cunt piece.

Women and men faint during the show. It happens a lot. Always at the exact same place in the script.

People bring and send objects—vagina products: vagina glass hand sculptures, clit lollipops, vagina puppets, vulva lamps, cone-shaped art pieces.

There is a huge vagina cake in London at the V-Day party and no one can cut it. Hundreds of sophisticated partygoers eat mauve vagina cake with their hands. The clit is auctioned off and Thandie Newton buys it for two hundred pounds.

The Vagina Monologues opens and is published in over twenty countries, including China and Turkey.

V-Day has an impossible time raising money from corporations. Even companies that sell vaginal products refuse to associate with the word.

Women call up for tickets to the "Monologues"; men ask for tickets to the "Vagina Chronicles." The punk ticketseller tells women that if they can't say it, they can't come.

A young corporate woman bursts into my dressing room to tell me she really isn't dry. It's a lie.

Two older Israeli women rush my dressing room in Jerusalem and hug me while I'm naked. They don't even notice.

A seventy-year-old man in a trance walks into my dressing room unannounced after a show to tell me that he "finally got it." Two months later he brings his girlfriend back with him and she thanks me.

Midwives storm the dressing room to thank me for finally appreciating bodily excretions.

A drag queen performs *TVM* on closing night.

Vagina miracles, sightings, and occurrences. They go on. The greatest miracle, of course, is V-Day: an energy, a movement, a catalyst, a day to end violence toward women—born out of *The Vagina Monologues.*

As I traveled with the piece to city after city, country after country, hundreds of women waited after the show to talk to me about their lives. The play had somehow freed up their memories, pain, and desire. Night after night I heard the same stories—women being raped as teenagers, in college, as little girls, as elderly women; women who had finally escaped being beaten to death by their husbands; women who were terrified to leave; women who were taken sexually, before they were even conscious of sex, by their stepfathers, brothers, cousins, uncles, mothers, and fathers. I began to feel insane, as if a door had opened to some underworld and I was being told things I was not supposed to know; knowing these things was dangerous.

Slowly, it dawned on me that nothing was

more important than stopping violence toward women—that the desecration of women indicated the failure of human beings to honor and protect life and that this failing would, if we did not correct it, be the end of us all. I do not think I am being extreme. When you rape, beat, maim, mutilate, burn, bury, and terrorize women, you destroy the essential life energy on the planet. You force what is meant to be open, trusting, nurturing, creative, and alive to be bent, infertile, and broken.

In 1997, I met with a group of activist women, many from a group called Feminst.com, and we formed V-Day. As with all the mysterious vagina happenings, we show up, we do the groundwork, we stay in shape, and the Vagina Queens do the rest. On February 14, 1998, Valentine's Day, our first V-Day was born. Twenty-five hundred people lined up outside the Hammerstein Ballroom in New York City for our first outrageous event. Whoopi Goldberg, Susan Sarandon, Glenn Close, Winona Ryder, Marisa Tomei, Shirley Knight, Lois Smith, Kathy Najimy, Calista Flockhart, Lily Tomlin, Hazelle Goodman, Margaret Cho, Hannah Ensler-Rivel, BETTY, Klezmer Women, Ulali, Phoebe Snow, Gloria Steinem, Soraya Mire, and Rosie Perez joined together to perform *The Vagina Monologues* and created a transforming evening that raised over $100,000 and launched the V-Day movement. Since then there have been stellar events at the Old Vic in London in 1999, with performers including Cate Blanchett, Kate Winslet, Melanie Griffith, Meera Syal, Julia Sawalha, Joely Richardson, Ruby Wax, Eddi Reader, Katie Puckrik, Dani Behr, Natasha McElhone, Sophie Dahl, Jane Lapotaire, Thandie Newton, and Gillian Anderson. In 2000, V-Day was celebrated in Los Angeles, Santa Fe, Sarasota, Aspen, and Chicago.

In three years, V-Day has happened at over three hundred colleges, with performances of *The Vagina Monologues* directed and performed by students and faculty. All the productions raise money and consciousness for local groups that work to stop violence toward women.

The Off-Broadway production of *The Vagina Monologues* will raise nearly $1 million for V-Day. Subsequent productions around the country and the world will support the movement as well.

At this point, the V-Day Fund is supporting grassroots groups around the world, where, in several cases, women are fighting with their lives to protect women and end the violence. In Afghanistan, there is RAWA, Revolutionary Association of the Women of Afghanistan, a group devoted to liberating women from the terrible oppression of the Taliban. There, women are not allowed to work, to be educated, to go to the doctor, or to leave their house without a male escort. There, women are being buried under their burqas without any protection from rape or murder. The V-Day Fund is helping RAWA educate women in clandestine schools, documenting illegal executions, and building a women's movement. In Kenya, Africa, we are supporting Tasaru Ntomonok (Safe Motherhood Initiative), part of Mandeolo—a project that is stopping the practice of young girls being genitally mutilated by introducing a new coming-of-age ritual without the cut. Recently, we were able to buy them a red jeep so they can travel more easily from village to village as they continue the education and prevention. In Croatia, we are working with the Center for Women War Victims, which through our support will open the first rape crisis center in the former Yugoslavia. The center will also be able to train women in Kosova and Chechyna to work with women in those countries who have been raped and traumatized during the war. V-Day is working in collaboration with Planned Parenthood to implement within their already existing programs a strategy to prevent and end violence toward women. The list goes on and on.

The miracle of V-Day, like *The Vagina Monologues,* is that it happened because it had to happen. A call, perhaps; an unconscious mandate, perhaps. I surrender to the Vagina Queens.

Something is unfolding. It is both mystical

and practical. It requires that we show up, do our exercise, and get out of the way.

In order for the human race to continue, women must be safe and empowered. It's an obvious idea, but like a vagina, it needs great attention and love in order to be revealed.

THE
VAGINA
MONOLOGUES

I bet you're worried. *I* was worried. That's why I began this piece. I was worried about vaginas. I was worried about what we think about vaginas, and even more worried that we don't think about them. I was worried about my own vagina. It needed a context of other vaginas—a community, a culture of vaginas. There's so much darkness and secrecy surrounding them—like the

Bermuda Triangle. Nobody ever reports back from there.

In the first place, it's not so easy even to find your vagina. Women go weeks, months, sometimes years without looking at it. I interviewed a high-powered businesswoman who told me she was too busy; she didn't have the time. Looking at your vagina, she said, is a full day's work. You have to get down there on your back in front of a mirror that's standing on its own, full-length preferred. You've got to get in the perfect position, with the perfect light, which then is shadowed somehow by the mirror and the angle you're at. You get all twisted up. You're arching your head up, killing your back. You're exhausted by then. She said she didn't have the time for that. She was busy.

So I decided to talk to women about their vaginas, to do vagina interviews, which became vagina monologues. I talked with over two hundred women. I talked to older women, young women, married women, single women, lesbians, college professors, actors, corporate professionals, sex workers, African American women, Hispanic women, Asian American women, Native American women, Caucasian women, Jewish women. At first women were reluctant to talk. They were a little shy. But once they got going, you couldn't stop them. Women secretly love to talk about their vaginas. They get very excited, mainly because no one's ever asked them before.

Let's just start with the word "vagina." It sounds like an infection at best, maybe a medical instrument: "Hurry, Nurse, bring me the vagina." "Vagina." "Vagina." Doesn't matter how many times you say it, it never sounds like a word you want to say. It's a totally ridiculous, completely unsexy word. If you use it during sex, trying to be politically correct—"Darling, could you stroke my vagina?"—you kill the act right there.

I'm worried about vaginas, what we call them and don't call them.

In Great Neck, they call it a pussycat. A woman there told me that her mother used to tell

her, "Don't wear panties underneath your pajamas, dear; you need to air out your pussycat." In
Westchester they called it a pooki, in New Jersey
a twat. There's "powderbox," "derrière," a
"poochi," a "poopi," a "peepe," a "poopelu," a
"poonani," a "pal" and a "piche," "toadie," "dee
dee," "nishi," "dignity," "monkey box," "coochi
snorcher," "cooter," "labbe," "Gladys Siegelman,"
"VA," "wee wee," "horsespot," "nappy dugout,"
"mongo," a "pajama," "fannyboo," "mushmel-
low," a "ghoulie," "possible," "tamale," "tottita,"
"Connie," a "Mimi" in Miami, "split knish" in
Philadelphia, and "schmende" in the Bronx. I am
worried about vaginas.

Some of the monologues are close to verbatim interviews, some are composite interviews, and with some I just began with the seed of an interview and had a good time. This monologue is pretty much the way I heard it. Its subject, however, came up in every interview, and often it was fraught. The subject being

H A I R

You cannot love a vagina unless you love hair. Many people do not love hair. My first and only husband hated hair. He said it was cluttered and dirty. He made me shave my vagina. It looked puffy and exposed and like a little girl. This excited him. When he made love to me, my vagina felt the way a beard must feel. It felt good to rub it, and painful. Like scratching a mosquito bite. It felt like it was on fire. There were screaming red bumps. I refused to shave it again. Then my husband had an affair. When we went to marital therapy, he said he screwed around because I wouldn't please him sexually. I wouldn't shave my vagina. The therapist had a thick German accent and gasped between sentences to show her empathy. She asked me why I didn't want to please my husband. I told her I thought it was weird. I felt little when my hair was gone down there, and I couldn't help talking in a baby voice, and the skin got irritated and even calamine lotion wouldn't help it. She told me marriage was a compromise. I asked her if shaving my vagina would stop him from screwing around. I asked her if she'd had many cases like this before. She said that questions diluted the process. I needed to jump in. She was sure it was a good beginning.

This time, when we got home, he got to shave my vagina. It was like a therapy bonus prize. He clipped it a few times, and there was a little blood in the bathtub. He didn't even notice it, 'cause he was so happy shaving me. Then, later, when my husband was pressing against me, I could feel his spiky sharpness sticking into me, my naked puffy vagina. There was no protection. There was no fluff.

I realized then that hair is there for a reason—it's the leaf around the flower, the lawn around the house. You have to love hair in order to love the vagina. You can't pick the parts you want. And besides, my husband never stopped screwing around.

I asked all the women I interviewed the same questions and then I picked my favorite answers. Although I must tell you, I've never heard an answer I didn't love. I asked women:

"If your vagina got dressed, what would it wear?"

A beret.

A leather jacket.

Silk stockings.

Mink.

A pink boa.

A male tuxedo.

Jeans.

Something formfitting.

Emeralds.

An evening gown.

Sequins.

Armani only.

A tutu.

See-through black underwear.

A taffeta ball gown.

Something machine washable.

Costume eye mask.

Purple velvet pajamas.

Angora.

A red bow.

Ermine and pearls.

A large hat full of flowers.

A leopard hat.

A silk kimono.

Glasses.

Sweatpants.

A tattoo.

An electrical shock device to keep unwanted
strangers away.

High heels.

Lace *and* combat boots.

Purple feathers and twigs and shells.

Cotton.

A pinafore.

A bikini.

A slicker.

"If your vagina could talk, what would it say, in two words?"

Slow down.

Is that you?

Feed me.

I want.

Yum, yum.

Oh, yeah.

Start again.

No, over there.

Lick me.

Stay home.

Brave choice.

Think again.

More, please.

Embrace me.

Let's play.

Don't stop.

More, more.

Remember me?

Come inside.

Not yet.

Whoah, Mama.

Yes yes.

Rock me.

Enter at your own risk.

Oh, God.

Thank God.

I'm here.

Let's go.

Let's go.

Find me.

Thank you.

Bonjour.

Too hard.

Don't give up.

Where's Brian?

That's better.

Yes, there. There.

I interviewed a group of women between the ages of sixty-five and seventy-five. These interviews were the most poignant of all, possibly because many of the women had never had a vagina interview before. Unfortunately, most of the women in this age group had very little conscious relationship to their vaginas. I felt terribly lucky to have grown up in the feminist era. One woman who was seventy-two had never even seen her vagina. She had only touched herself when she was

washing in the shower, but never with conscious inten-tion. She had never had an orgasm. At seventy-two she went into therapy, and with the encouragement of her therapist, she went home one afternoon by herself, lit some candles, took a bath, played some comforting music, and discovered her vagina. She said it took her over an hour, because she was arthritic by then, but when she finally found her clitoris, she said, she cried. This monologue is for her.

T H E   F L O O D

[Jewish, Queens accent]

Down there? I haven't been down there since 1953. No, it had nothing to do with Eisenhower. No, no, it's a cellar down there. It's very damp, clammy. You don't want to go down there. Trust me. You'd get sick. Suffocating. Very nauseating. The smell of the clamminess and the mildew and everything. Whew! Smells unbearable. Gets in your clothes.

No, there was no accident down there. It

didn't blow up or catch on fire or anything. It wasn't so dramatic. I mean . . . well, never mind. No. Never mind. I can't talk to you about this. What's a smart girl like you going around talking to old ladies about their down-theres for? We didn't do this kind of a thing when I was a girl. What? Jesus, okay.

There was this boy, Andy Leftkov. He was cute—well, I thought so. And tall, like me, and I really liked him. He asked me out for a date in his car. . . .

I can't tell you this. I can't do this, talk about down there. You just know it's there. Like the cellar. There's rumbles down there sometimes. You can hear the pipes, and things get caught there, little animals and things, and it gets wet, and sometimes people have to come and plug up the leaks. Otherwise, the door stays closed. You forget about it. I mean, it's part of the house, but you don't see it or think about it. It has to be there, though, 'cause every house needs a cellar. Otherwise the bedroom would be in the basement.

Oh, Andy, Andy Leftkov. Right. Andy was very good-looking. He was a catch. That's what we called it in my day. We were in his car, a new white Chevy BelAir. I remember thinking that my legs were too long for the seat. I have long legs. They were bumping up against the dashboard. I was looking at my big kneecaps when he just kissed me in this surprisingly "Take me by control like they do in the movies" kind of way. And I got excited, so excited, and, well, there was a flood down there. I couldn't control it. It was like this force of passion, this river of life just flooded out of me, right through my panties, right onto the car seat of his new white Chevy BelAir. It wasn't pee and it was smelly—well, frankly, I didn't really smell anything at all, but he said, Andy said, that it smelled like sour milk and it was staining his car seat. I was "a stinky weird girl," he said. I wanted to explain that his kiss had caught me off guard, that I wasn't normally like this. I tried to wipe the flood up with my dress. It was a new yellow prim-rose dress and it looked so ugly with the flood on it. Andy drove me home and he never, never said another word and when I got out and closed his car door, I closed the whole store. Locked it. Never opened for business again. I dated some after that, but the idea of flooding made me too nervous. I never even got close again.

I used to have dreams, crazy dreams. Oh, they're dopey. Why? Burt Reynolds. I don't know why. He never did much for me in life, but in my dreams . . . it was always Burt and I. Burt and I. Burt and I. We'd be out. Burt and I. It was some restaurant like the kind you see in Atlantic City, all big with chandeliers and stuff and thousands of waiters with vests on. Burt would give me this orchid corsage. I'd pin it on my blazer. We'd laugh. We were always laughing, Burt and I. Eat shrimp cocktail. Huge shrimp, fabulous shrimp. We'd laugh more. We were very happy together. Then he'd look into my eyes and pull me to him in the middle of the restaurant—and, just as he was about to kiss me, the room would start to shake, pigeons would fly out from under the table—I don't know what those pigeons were doing there—and the flood would come straight from down there. It would pour out of me. It would pour and pour. There would be fish inside it, and little boats, and the whole restaurant would fill with water, and Burt would be standing knee-deep in my flood, looking horribly disappointed in me that I'd done it again, horrified as he watched his friends, Dean Martin and the like, swim past us in their tuxedos and evening gowns.

I don't have those dreams anymore. Not since they took away just about everything connected with down there. Moved out the uterus, the tubes, the whole works. The doctor thought he was being funny. He told me if you don't use it, you lose it. But really I found out it was cancer. Everything around it had to go. Who needs it, anyway? Right? Highly overrated. I've done other things. I love the dog shows. I sell antiques.

What would it wear? What kind of question is that? What would it wear? It would wear a big sign:

"Closed Due to Flooding."

What would it say? I told you. It's not like that. It's not like a person who speaks. It stopped being a thing that talked a long time ago. It's a place. A place you don't go. It's closed up, under the house. It's down there. You happy? You made me talk—you got it out of me. You got an old lady to talk about her down-there. You feel better now? [Turns away; turns back.]

You know, actually, you're the first person I ever talked to about this, and I feel a little better.

VAGINA FACT

At a witch trial in 1593, the investigating lawyer (a married man) apparently discovered a clitoris for the first time; [he] identified it as a devil's teat, sure proof of the witch's guilt. It was "a little lump of flesh, in manner sticking out as if it had been a teat, to the length of half an inch," which the gaoler, "perceiving at the first sight thereof, meant not to disclose, because it was adjoining to so secret a place which was not decent to be seen. Yet in the end, not willing to conceal so strange a matter," he showed it to various bystanders. The bystanders had never seen anything like it. The witch was convicted.

—*The Woman's Encyclopedia of Myths and Secrets*

I interviewed many women about menstruation. There was a choral thing that began to occur, a kind of wild collective song. Women echoed each other. I let the voices bleed into one another. I got lost in the bleeding.

I WAS TWELVE. MY MOTHER SLAPPED ME.

Second grade, seven years old, my brother was talking about periods. I didn't like the way he was laughing.

I went to my mother. "What's a period?" I said. "It's punctuation," she said. "You put it at the end of a sentence."

My father brought me a card: "To my little girl who isn't so little anymore."

I was terrified. My mother showed me the

thick sanitary napkins. I was to bring the used ones to the can under the kitchen sink.

I remember being one of the last. I was thirteen.

We all wanted it to come.

I was so afraid. I started putting the used pads in brown paper bags in the dark storage places under the roof.

Eighth grade. My mother said, "Oh, that's nice."

In junior high—brown drips before it came. Coincided with a little hair under my arms, which grew unevenly: one armpit had hair, the other didn't.

I was sixteen, sort of scared.

My mother gave me codeine. We had bunk beds. I went down and lay there. My mother was so uncomfortable.

One night, I came home late and snuck into bed without turning on any lights. My mother had found the used pads and put them between the sheets of my bed.

I was twelve years old, still in my underpants. Hadn't gotten dressed. Looked down on the staircase. There it was.

Looked down and I saw blood.

Seventh grade; my mother sort of noticed my underwear. Then she gave me plastic diapers.

My mom was very warm—"Let's get you a pad."

My friend Marcia, they celebrated when she got hers. They had dinner for her.

We all wanted our period.

We all wanted it *now*.

Thirteen years old. It was before Kotex. Had to watch your dress. I was black and poor. Blood on the back of my dress in church. Didn't show, but I was guilty.

I was ten and a half. No preparation. Brown gunk on my underpants.

She showed me how to put in a tampon. Only got in halfway.

I associated my period with inexplicable phenomena.

My mother told me I had to use a rag. My mother said no to tampons. You couldn't put anything in your sugar dish.

Wore wads of cotton. Told my mother. She gave me Elizabeth Taylor paper dolls.

Fifteen years old. My mother said, "Mazel tov." She slapped me in the face. Didn't know if it was a good thing or a bad thing.

My period, like cake mix before it's baked. Indians sat on moss for five days. Wish I were Native American.

I was fifteen and I'd been hoping to get it. I was tall and I kept growing.

When I saw white girls in the gym with tampons, I thought they were bad girls.

Saw little red drops on the pink tiles. I said, "Yeah."

My mom was glad for me.

Used OB and liked putting my fingers up there.

Eleven years old, wearing white pants. Blood started to come out.

Thought it was dreadful.

I'm not ready.

I got back pains.

I got horny.

Twelve years old. I was happy. My friend had a Ouija board, asked when we were going to get our periods, looked down, and I saw blood.

Looked down and there it was.

I'm a woman.

Terrified.

Never thought it would come.

Changed my whole feeling about myself. I became very silent and mature. A good Vietnamese woman—quiet worker, virtuous, never speaks.

Nine and a half. I was sure I was bleeding to death, rolled up my underwear and threw them in a corner. Didn't want to worry my parents.

My mother made me hot water and wine, and I fell asleep.

I was in my bedroom in my mother's apartment. I had a comic book collection. My mother said, "You mustn't lift your box of comic books."

My girlfriends told me you hemorrhage every month.

My mother was in and out of mental hospitals. She couldn't take me coming of age.

"Dear Miss Carling, Please excuse my daughter from basketball. She has just matured."

At camp they told me not to take a bath with my period. They wiped me down with antiseptic.

Scared people would smell it. Scared they'd say I smelled like fish.

Throwing up, couldn't eat.

I got hungry.

Sometimes it's very red.

I like the drops that drop into the toilet. Like paint.

Sometimes it's brown and it disturbs me.

I was twelve. My mother slapped me and brought me a red cotton shirt. My father went out for a bottle of sangria.

Over the course of my interviews I met nine women who had had their first orgasms in the exact same place. They were women in their late thirties and early forties. They had all participated, at different times, in one of the groups run by a brave and extraordinary woman, Betty Dodson. For twenty-five years Betty has been helping women locate, love, and masturbate their vaginas. She has run groups, has worked privately with individual women. She has helped thousands of women reclaim their center. This piece is for her.

THE

VAGINA

WORKSHOP

[A slight English accent]

My vagina is a shell, a round pink tender shell, opening and closing, closing and opening. My vagina is a flower, an eccentric tulip, the center acute and deep, the scent delicate, the petals gentle but sturdy.

I did not always know this. I learned this in the vagina workshop. I learned this from a woman who runs the vagina workshop, a woman who believes in vaginas, who really sees vaginas, who helps women see their own vaginas by seeing other women's vaginas.

In the first session the woman who runs the vagina workshop asked us to draw a picture of our own "unique, beautiful, fabulous vagina." That's what she called it. She wanted to know what our own unique, beautiful, fabulous vagina looked like to us. One woman who was pregnant drew a big red mouth screaming with coins spilling out. Another very skinny woman drew a big serving plate with a kind of Devonshire pattern on it. I drew a huge black dot with little squiggly lines around it. The black dot was equal to a black hole in space, and the squiggly lines were meant to be people or things or just your basic atoms that got lost there. I had always thought of my vagina as an anatomical vacuum randomly sucking up particles and objects from the surrounding environment.

I had always perceived my vagina as an independent entity, spinning like a star in its own galaxy, eventually burning up on its own gaseous energy or exploding and splitting into thousands of other smaller vaginas, all of them then spinning in their own galaxies.

I did not think of my vagina in practical or biological terms. I did not, for example, see it as a part of my body, something between my legs, attached to me.

In the workshop we were asked to look at our vaginas with hand mirrors. Then, after careful examination, we were to verbally report to the group what we saw. I must tell you that up until this point everything I knew about my vagina was based on hearsay or invention. I had never really seen the thing. It had never occurred to me to look at it. My vagina existed for me on some abstract plane. It seemed so reductive and awkward to look at it, getting down there the way we did in the workshop, on our shiny blue mats, with our hand mirrors. It reminded me of how the early astronomers must have felt with their primitive telescopes.

I found it quite unsettling at first, my vagina.

Like the first time you see a fish cut open and you discover this other bloody complex world inside, right under the skin. It was so raw, so red, so fresh. And the thing that surprised me most was all the layers. Layers inside layers, opening into more layers.

My vagina amazed me. I couldn't speak when it came my turn in the workshop. I was speechless. I had awakened to what the woman who ran the workshop called "vaginal wonder." I just wanted to lie there on my mat, my legs spread, examining my vagina forever.

It was better than the Grand Canyon, ancient and full of grace. It had the innocence and freshness of a proper English garden. It was funny, very funny. It made me laugh. It could hide and seek, open and close. It was a mouth. It was the morning.

Then, the woman who ran the workshop asked how many women in the workshop had had orgasms. Two women tentatively raised their hands. I didn't raise my hand, but I had had orgasms. I didn't raise my hand because they were accidental orgasms. They happened *to* me. They happened in my dreams, and I would wake in splendor. They happened a lot in water, mostly in the bath. Once in Cape Cod. They happened on horses, on bicycles, on the treadmill at the gym. I did not raise my hand because although I had had orgasms, I did not know how to make one happen. I had never tried to make one happen. I thought it was a mystical, magical thing. I didn't want to interfere. It felt wrong, getting involved—contrived, manipulative. It felt Hollywood. Orgasms by formula. The surprise would be gone, and the mystery. The problem, of course, was that the surprise had been gone for two years. I hadn't had a magical accidental orgasm in a long time, and I was frantic. That's why I was in the workshop.

And then the moment had arrived that I both dreaded and secretly longed for. The woman who ran the workshop asked us to take out our hand mirrors again and to see if we could locate our clitoris. We were there, the group of us women, on our backs, on our mats, finding our spots, our locus, our reason, and I don't know why, but I started crying. Maybe it was sheer embarrassment. Maybe it was knowing that I had to give up the fantasy, the enormous life-consuming fantasy, that someone or something was going to do this for me—the fantasy that someone was coming to lead my life, to choose direction, to give me orgasms. I was used to living off the record, in a magical, superstitious way. This clitoris finding, this wild workshop on shiny blue mats, was making the whole thing real, too real. I could feel the panic coming. The simultaneous terror and realization that I had avoided finding my clitoris, had rationalized it as mainstream and consumerist because I was, in fact, terrified that I did not *have* a clitoris, terrified that I was one of those constitutionally incapables, one of those frigid, dead, shut-down, dry, apricot-tasting, bitter—oh, my God. I lay there with my mirror looking for my spot, reaching with my fingers, and all

I could think about was the time when I was ten and lost my gold ring with the emeralds in a lake. How I kept diving over and over to the bottom of the lake, running my hands over stones and fish and bottle caps and slimy stuff, but never my ring. The panic I felt. I knew I'd be punished. I shouldn't have worn it swimming.

The woman who ran the workshop saw my insane scrambling, sweating, and heavy breathing. She came over. I told her, "I've lost my clitoris. It's gone. I shouldn't have worn it swimming." The woman who ran the workshop laughed. She calmly stroked my forehead. She told me my clitoris was not something I could lose. It was me, the essence of me. It was both the doorbell to my house and the house itself. I didn't have to *find* it. I had to *be* it. Be it. Be my clitoris. Be my clitoris. I lay back and closed my eyes. I put the mirror down. I watched myself float above myself. I watched as I slowly began to approach myself and reenter. I felt like an astronaut reentering the atmosphere of the earth. It was very quiet, this reentry: quiet and gentle. I bounced and landed, landed and bounced. I came into my own muscles and blood and cells and then I just slid into my vagina. It was suddenly easy and I fit. I was all warm and pulsing and ready and young and alive. And then, without looking, with my eyes still closed, I put my finger on what had suddenly become me. There was a little quivering at first, which urged me to stay. Then the quivering became a quake, an eruption, the layers dividing and subdividing. The quaking broke open into an ancient horizon of light and silence, which opened onto a plane of music and colors and innocence and longing, and I felt connection, calling connection as I lay there thrashing about on my little blue mat.

My vagina is a shell, a tulip, and a destiny. I am arriving as I am beginning to leave. My vagina, my vagina, me.

VAGINA FACT

The clitoris is pure in purpose. It is the only organ in the body designed purely for pleasure. The clitoris is simply a bundle of nerves: 8,000 nerve fibers, to be precise. That's a higher concentration of nerve fibers than is found anywhere else in the body, including the fingertips, lips, and tongue, and it is twice . . . twice . . . twice the number in the penis. Who needs a handgun when you've got a semiautomatic.

—from *Woman: An Intimate Geography,* by Natalie Angier

BECAUSE HE LIKED TO LOOK AT IT

This is how I came to love my vagina. It's embarrassing, because it's not politically correct. I mean, I know it should have happened in a bath with salt grains from the Dead Sea, Enya playing, me loving my woman self. I know the story. Vaginas are beautiful. Our self-hatred is only the internalized repression and hatred of the patriarchal culture. It isn't real. Pussys unite. I know all of it. Like, if we'd grown up in a culture where we were taught that fat thighs were beautiful, we'd all be pounding down milkshakes and cookies, lying on our backs, spending our days thigh-expanding. But we didn't grow up in that culture. I hated my thighs, and I hated my vagina even more. I thought it was incredibly ugly. I was one of those women who had looked at it and, from that moment on, wished I hadn't. It made me sick. I pitied anyone who had to go down there.

In order to survive, I began to pretend there was something else between my legs. I imagined furniture—cozy futons with light cotton comforters, little velvet settees, leopard rugs—or pretty things—silk handkerchiefs, quilted pot holders, or place settings—or miniature landscapes—clear crystal lakes or moisty Irish bogs. I got so accustomed to this that I lost all memory of having a vagina. Whenever I had sex with a man, I pictured him inside a mink-lined muffler or a red rose or a Chinese bowl.

Then I met Bob. Bob was the most ordinary man I ever met. He was thin and tall and nondescript and wore khaki clothes. Bob did not like spicy foods or listen to Prodigy. He had no interest in sexy lingerie. In the summer he spent time in the shade. He did not share his inner feelings. He did not have any problems or issues, and was not even an alcoholic. He wasn't very funny or articulate or mysterious. He wasn't mean or unavailable. He wasn't self-involved or charismatic. He didn't drive fast. I didn't particularly like Bob. I would have missed him altogether if he hadn't picked up my change that I dropped on the deli floor. When he handed me back my quarters and pennies and his hand accidentally touched mine, something happened. I went to bed with him. That's when the miracle occurred.

Turned out that Bob loved vaginas. He was a connoisseur. He loved the way they felt, the way they tasted, the way they smelled, but most important, he loved the way they looked. He had to look at them. The first time we had sex, he told me he had to see me.

"I'm right here," I said.

"No, you," he said. "I have to see you."

"Turn on the light," I said.

Thinking he was a weirdo, I was freaking out in the dark. He turned on the light.

Then he said, "Okay. I'm ready, ready to see you."

"Right here." I waved. "I'm right here."

Then he began to undress me.

"What are you doing, Bob?" I said.

"I need to see you," he replied.

"No need," I said. "Just dive in."

"I need to see what you look like," he said.

"But you've seen a red leather couch before," I said.

Bob continued. He would not stop. I wanted to throw up and die.

"This is awfully intimate," I said. "Can't you just dive in?"

"No," he said. "It's who you are. I need to look."

I held my breath. He looked and looked. He gasped and smiled and stared and groaned. He got breathy and his face changed. He didn't look ordinary anymore. He looked like a hungry, beautiful beast.

"You're so beautiful," he said. "You're elegant and deep and innocent and wild."

"You saw that there?" I said.

It was like he read my palm.

"I saw that," he said, "and more—much, much more."

He stayed looking for almost an hour, as if he were studying a map, observing the moon, staring into my eyes, but it was my vagina. In the light, I watched him looking at me, and he was so genuinely excited, so peaceful and euphoric, I began to get wet and turned on. I began to see myself the way he saw me. I began to feel beautiful and delicious—like a great painting or a waterfall. Bob wasn't afraid. He wasn't grossed out. I began to swell, began to feel proud. Began to love my vagina. And Bob lost himself there and I was there with him, in my vagina, and we were gone.

In 1993, I was walking down a street in Manhattan when I passed a newsstand and was suddenly struck by a deeply disturbing photograph on the front page of Newsday. *It was a picture of a group of six young women who had just been returned from a rape camp in Bosnia. Their faces revealed shock and despair, but more disturbing was a sense that something sweet, something pure, had been forever destroyed in each of their lives. I read on. Inside the newspaper was another photograph of the young women, recently reunited with*

their mothers and standing in a semicircle in a gymna-sium. There was a very large group and not one of them, mother or daughter, was able to look at the camera.

I knew I had to go there. I had to meet these women. In 1994, thanks to the support of an angel, Lauren Lloyd, I spent two months in Croatia and Pak-istan, interviewing Bosnian women refugees. I inter-viewed these women and hung out with them in camps, cafés, and refugee centers. I have been back to Bosnia twice since then.

When I returned to New York after my first trip, I was in a state of outrage. Outraged that 20,000 to 70,000 women were being raped in the middle of Eu-rope in 1993, as a systematic tactic of war, and no one was doing anything to stop it. I couldn't understand it. A friend asked me why I was surprised. She said that over 500,000 women were raped every year in this country, and in theory we were not at war.

This monologue is based on one woman's story. I want to thank her here for sharing it with me. I am in awe of her spirit and strength, as I am in awe of every woman I met who survived these terrible atrocities in the former Yugoslavia. This piece is for the women of Bosnia.

MY VAGINA WAS MY

VILLAGE

My vagina was green, water soft pink fields,
cow mooing sun resting sweet boyfriend touching
lightly with soft piece of blond straw.

There is something between my legs. I do not know
what it is. I do not know where it is. I do not touch. Not
now. Not anymore. Not since.

My vagina was chatty, can't wait, so much,
so much saying, words talking, can't quit trying,
can't quit saying, oh yes, oh yes.

Not since I dream there's a dead animal sewn in down there with thick black fishing line. And the bad dead animal smell cannot be removed. And its throat is slit and it bleeds through all my summer dresses.

My vagina singing all girl songs, all goat bells ringing songs, all wild autumn field songs, vagina songs, vagina home songs.

Not since the soldiers put a long thick rifle inside me. So cold, the steel rod canceling my heart. Don't know whether they're going to fire it or shove it through my spinning brain. Six of them, monstrous doctors with black masks shoving bottles up me too. There were sticks, and the end of a broom.

My vagina swimming river water, clean spilling water over sun-baked stones over stone clit, clit stones over and over.

Not since I heard the skin tear and made lemon screeching sounds, not since a piece of my vagina came off in my hand, a part of the lip, now one side of the lip is completely gone.

My vagina. A live wet water village. My vagina my hometown.

Not since they took turns for seven days smelling like feces and smoked meat, they left their dirty sperm inside me. I became a river of poison and pus and all the crops died, and the fish.

My vagina a live wet water village.
They invaded it. Butchered it and burned it
    down.
I do not touch now.
Do not visit.
I live someplace else now.
I don't know where that is.

VAGINA FACT

In the nineteenth century, girls who learned to develop orgasmic capacity by masturbation were regarded as medical problems. Often they were "treated" or "corrected" by amputation or cautery of the clitoris or "miniature chastity belts," sewing the vaginal lips together to put the clitoris out of reach, and even castration by surgical removal of the ovaries. But there are no references in the medical literature to the surgical removal of testicles or amputation of the penis to stop masturbation in boys.

In the United States, the last recorded clitoridectomy for curing masturbation was performed in 1948—on a five-year-old girl.

—*The Woman's Encyclopedia of Myths and Secrets*

Genital mutilation has been inflicted on 80 [million] to 100 million girls and young women. In countries where it is practiced, mostly African, about 2 million youngsters a year can expect the knife—or the razor or a glass shard—to cut their clitoris or remove it altogether, [and] to have part or all of the labia . . . sewn together with catgut or thorns.

Often the operation is prettified as "circumcision." The African specialist Nahid Toubia puts it plain: In a man it would range from amputation of most of the penis, to "removal of all the penis, its roots of soft tissue and part of the scrotal skin."

Short-term results include tetanus, septicemia, hemorrhages, cuts in the urethra, bladder, vaginal walls, and anal sphincter. Long-term: chronic uterine infection, massive scars that can hinder walking for life, fistula formation, hugely increased agony and danger during childbirth, and early deaths.

—*The New York Times*, April 12, 1996

MY ANGRY VAGINA

My vagina's angry. It is. It's pissed off. My vagina's furious and it needs to talk. It needs to talk about all this shit. It needs to talk to you. I mean, what's the deal? An army of people out there thinking up ways to torture my poor-ass, gentle, loving vagina. . . . Spending their days constructing psycho products and nasty ideas to undermine my pussy. Vagina motherfuckers.

All this shit they're constantly trying to

shove up us, clean us up—stuff us up, make it go away. Well, my vagina's not going away. It's pissed off and it's staying right here. Like tampons— what the hell is that? A wad of dry fucking cotton stuffed up there. Why can't they find a way to subtly lubricate the tampon? As soon as my vagina sees it, it goes into shock. It says, Forget it. It closes up. You need to work with the vagina, introduce it to things, prepare the way. That's what foreplay's all about. You got to convince my vagina, seduce my vagina, engage my vagina's trust. You can't do that with a dry wad of fucking cotton.

Stop shoving things up me. Stop shoving and stop cleaning it up. My vagina doesn't need to be cleaned up. It smells good already. Not like rose petals. Don't try to decorate. Don't believe him when he tells you it smells like rose petals when it's supposed to smell like pussy. That's what they're doing—trying to clean it up, make it smell like bathroom spray or a garden. All those douche sprays—floral, berry, rain. I don't want my pussy to smell like rain. All cleaned up like washing a fish after you cook it. Want to *taste* the fish. That's why I ordered it.

Then there's those exams. Who thought them up? There's got to be a better way to do those exams. Why the scary paper dress that scratches your tits and crunches when you lie down so you feel like a wad of paper someone threw away? Why the rubber gloves? Why the flashlight all up there like Nancy Drew working against gravity, why the Nazi steel stirrups, the mean cold duck lips they shove inside you? What's that? My vagina's angry about those visits. It gets defended weeks in advance. It shuts down, won't "relax." Don't you hate that? "Relax your vagina, relax your vagina." Why? My vagina's not stupid. Relax so you can shove those cold duck lips inside it? I don't think so.

Why can't they find some nice, delicious purple velvet and wrap it around me, lay me down on some feathery cotton spread, put on some nice, friendly pink or blue gloves, and rest my feet in some fur-covered stirrups? Warm up the duck lips. Work with my vagina.

But no, more tortures: dry wad of fucking cotton, cold duck lips, and thong underwear. That's the worst. Thong underwear. Who thought that up? Moves around all the time, gets stuck in the back of your vagina, real crusty butt.

Vagina's supposed to be loose and wide, not held together. That's why girdles are so bad. We need to move and spread and talk and talk. Vaginas need comfort. Make something like that, something to give them pleasure. No, of course they won't do that. Hate to see a woman having pleasure, particularly sexual pleasure. I mean, make a nice pair of soft cotton underwear with a French tickler built in. Women would be coming all day long, coming in the supermarket, coming on the subway, coming, happy vaginas. They wouldn't be able to stand it. Seeing all those energized, not-taking-shit, hot, happy vaginas.

If my vagina could talk, it would talk about itself like me; it would talk about other vaginas; it would do vagina impressions.

It would wear Harry Winston diamonds, no clothing—just there, all draped in diamonds.

My vagina helped release a giant baby. It thought it would be doing more of that. It's not. Now it wants to travel, doesn't want a lot of company. It wants to read and know things and get out more. It wants sex. It loves sex. It wants to go deeper. It's hungry for depth. It wants kindness. It wants change. It wants silence and freedom and gentle kisses and warm liquids and deep touch. It wants chocolate. It wants to scream. It wants to stop being angry. It wants to come. It wants to want. It wants. My vagina, my vagina. Well . . . it wants everything.

For the last ten years I have been actively involved with women who have no homes, women we call "homeless people" so we can categorize and forget them. I have done all kinds of things with these women, who have become my friends. I run recovery groups for women who have been raped or suffered incest, and groups for women addicted to drugs and alcohol. I go to the movies with these women, I have meals with them. I hang out. Over the past ten years I have interviewed hundreds of women. In all that time I have met only two who were

not subjected to incest as young girls or raped as young women. I have evolved a theory that for most of these women, "home" is a very scary place, a place they have fled, and that the shelters where I meet them are the first places many of them ever find safety, protection, or comfort, in the community of other women.

This monologue is one woman's story as she told it to me. I met her about five years ago, in a shelter. I would like to tell you it's an unusual story—brutal; extreme. But it's not. In fact, it's not nearly as disturbing as many of the stories I've heard in the years since. Poor women suffer terrible sexual violence that goes unreported. Because of their social class, these women do not have access to therapy or other methods of healing. Their repeated abuse ultimately eats away at their self-esteem, driving them to drugs, prostitution, AIDS, and in many cases, death. Fortunately, this particular story has a different outcome. This woman met another woman in that shelter, and they fell in love. Through their love, they got out of the shelter system and have a beautiful life together today. I wrote this piece for them, for their amazing spirits, for the women we do not see, who hurt and who need us.

THE LITTLE
COOCHI SNORCHER
THAT COULD

[Southern woman of color]

Memory: December 1965; Five Years Old

My mama tells me in a scary, loud, life-threatening voice to stop scratching my coochi snorcher. I become terrified that I've scratched it off down there. I do not touch myself again, even in the bath. I am afraid of the water getting in and filling me up so I explode. I put Band-Aids over my coochi snorcher to cover the hole, but they fall off in the water. I imagine a stopper, a bathtub plug up there to prevent things from entering me. I sleep with three pairs of happy heart-patterned cotton underpants underneath my snap-up pajamas. I still want to touch myself, but I don't.

Memory: Seven Years Old

Edgar Montane, who is ten, gets angry at me and punches me with all his might between my legs. It feels like he breaks my entire self. I limp home. I can't pee. My mama asks me what's wrong with my coochi snorcher, and when I tell her what Edgar did to me she yells at me and says never to let anyone touch me down there again. I try to explain he didn't touch it, Mama, he punched it.

Memory: Nine Years Old

I play on the bed, bouncing and falling, and impale my coochi snorcher on the bedpost. I make high-pitched screamy noises that come straight from my coochi snorcher's mouth. I get taken to the hospital and they sew it up down there from where it's been torn apart.

Memory: Ten Years Old

I'm at my father's house and he's having a party upstairs. Everyone's drinking. I'm playing alone in the basement and I'm trying on my new white cotton bra and panties that my father's girl-friend gave me. Suddenly my father's best friend, this big man Alfred, comes up from behind and pulls my new underpants down and sticks his big hard penis into my coochi scorcher. I scream. I kick. I try to fight him off, but he already gets it in. My father's there then and he has a gun and there's a loud horrible noise and then there's blood all over Alfred and me, lots of blood. I'm sure my coochi snorcher is finally falling out. Al-fred is paralyzed for life and my mama doesn't let me see my father for seven years.

Memory: Twelve Years Old

My coochi snorcher is a very bad place, a place of pain, nastiness, punching, invasion, and blood. It's a site for mishaps. It's a bad-luck zone. I imagine a freeway between my legs and, girl, I am traveling, going far away from here.

Memory: Thirteen Years Old

There's this gorgeous twenty-four-year-old woman in our neighborhood and I stare at her all the time. One day she invites me into her car. She asks me if I like to kiss boys, and I tell her I do not like that. Then she says she wants to show me something, and she leans over and kisses me so softly on the lips with her lips and then puts her tongue in my mouth. Wow. She asks me if I want to come over to her house, and then she kisses me again and tells me to relax, to feel it, to let our tongues feel it. She asks my mama if I can spend the night and my mother's delighted that such a beautiful, successful woman has taken an interest in me. I'm scared but really I can't wait. Her apartment's fantastic. She's got it hooked up. It's the seventies: the beads, the fluffy pillows, the mood lights. I decide right there that I want to be a secretary like her when I grow up. She makes a vodka for herself and then she asks what I want to drink. I say the same as she's drinking and she says she doesn't think my mama would like me drinking vodka. I say she probably wouldn't like me kissing girls, either, and the pretty lady makes me a drink. Then she changes into this chocolate satin teddy. She's so beautiful. I always thought bulldaggers were ugly. I say, "You look great," and she says, "So do you." I say, "But I only have this white cotton bra and underpants." Then she dresses me, slowly, in another satin teddy. It's lavender like the first soft days of spring. The alcohol has gone to my head and I'm loose and ready. I noticed that there's a picture over her bed of a naked black woman with a huge afro as she gently and slowly lays me out on the bed. And just our bodies rubbing makes me come. Then she does everything. to me and my coochi snorcher that I always thought was nasty before, and wow. I'm so hot, so wild. She says, "Your vagina, untouched by man, smells so nice, so fresh, wish I could keep it that way forever." I get crazy wild and then the phone rings and of course it's my mama. I'm sure she knows; she catches me at everything. I'm breathing so heavy and I try to act normal when I get on the phone and she asks me, "What's wrong with you, have you been running?" I say, "No, Mama, exercising." Then she tells the beautiful secretary to make sure I'm not around boys and the lady tells her, "Trust me, there's no boys around here." Afterward the gorgeous lady teaches me everything about my coochi snorcher. She makes me play with myself in front of her and she teaches me all the different ways to give myself pleasure. She's very thorough. She tells me to always know how to give myself pleasure so I'll never need to rely on a man. In the morning I am worried that I've become a butch because I'm so in love with her. She laughs, but I never see her again. I realized later she was my surprising, unexpected, politically incorrect salvation. She transformed my sorry-ass coochi snorcher and raised it up into a kind of heaven.

During the course of my run in New York, I received this letter:

As the honorary chair of the Vulva Club, we would be more than pleased to make you a member. However, when Harriet Lerner developed this club over twenty years ago, membership was predicated on the understanding and correct usage of the word *vulva* and being able to communicate that to as many people as possible, especially women.

Warm regards,

Jane Hirschman

THE VULVA CLUB

I have always been obsessed with naming things. If I could name them, I could know them. If I could name them, I could tame them. They could be my friends.

For example, I had a large collection of frogs when I was a little girl: stuffed frogs, china frogs, plastic frogs, neon frogs, happy battery-operated frogs. Each one had a name. I took time to know them for a while before I named them. I sat them on my bed and would watch them in daylight, wear them in my coat pocket, hold them in my sweaty little hands. I came to know them by their texture, their smell, their shape, their size, their sense of humor. Then they would get named, usually in a splendid naming ceremony. Surrounding them with their frog friends, I would dress them in ceremonial coats, put sparkles on them, or gold stars, stand them in front of the frog chapel, and name them.

First, I would whisper the coveted name into their ear. *(whispering)* "You are my Froggie Doodle Mashy Pie." I would make sure the frog accepted the name. Then I would say it out loud for the other excited frogs, some of whom were waiting for their own names. "Froggie Doodle Mashy Pie." Then there would be singing, usually the name repeated over and over, joined by the other frogs. *(make up a song)* "Froggie Doodle Mashy Pie. Froggie Doodle Mashy Pie." This would happen with dancing.

I would line the froggies up and dance in and out of them, hopping like a frog and making general frog noises, always holding the newly christened frog in my hands or arms, depending on the size. It was an exhausting ceremony, but crucial. It would have been fine if it had been limited to frogs, but soon I needed to name everything. I named rugs and doors and chairs and stairs. Ben, for example, was my flashlight, named after my kindergarten teacher, who was always in my business.

I eventually named all the parts of my body. My hands—Gladys. They seemed functional and basic, like Gladys. I named my shoulders Shorty—strong and a little belligerent. My breasts were Betty. They weren't Veronica, but they weren't ugly either. Naming my "down there" was not so easy. It wasn't the same as naming my hands. No, it was complicated. Down there was alive, not so easy to pinpoint. It remained unnamed and, as unnamed, it was untamed, unknown.

We had a baby-sitter around then, Sara Stanley. She talked in this high-pitched voice that made me pee. When I was taking a bath one night, she told me to be sure to wash my "Itsy Bitsy." I can't say that I liked this name. It took a while even to figure out what it was. But there was something about her voice. The name stuck. Yes, there it is, my Itsy Bitsy.

Unfortunately, this name followed me into adulthood. On our first night in bed, I informed the man I would later marry that Itsy Bitsy was a little shy but eager, and if he would be patient, she would surely reveal her mysteries. He was a bit freaked out, I think, but as is his nature, he went along with it and later would actually call her by name. "Is Itsy Bitsy there? Is she ready?" I myself was never happy with her name, and so what happened later is not really surprising.

One night, my husband and I were in the act. He called out to her, "Come here, my little Itsy Bitsy," and she did not respond. It was as if she suddenly wasn't there. "Itsy Bitsy, it's me, your biggest fan." No word. No motion. So I called to her.

"Itsy Bitsy, come on out. Don't do this to me."

Not a word, not a sound. Itsy was dead and mute and gone.

"Itsy Bitsy!"

For days she did not come, then weeks, then months. I became despondent.

I reluctantly told my friend Teresa, who was spending all her time in this new women's group. I said, "Itsy Bitsy will not speak to me, Teresa. She won't return my calls."

"Who is Itsy Bitsy?"

"My Bitsy," I said. "My Itsy."

"What are you talking about?" she said in a voice that suddenly sounded much deeper than mine. "You mean your vulva, girl?"

"Vulva," I said to Teresa. "What exactly is that?"

"It's the package," she said. "It's the entire deal."

Vulva. Vulva. I could feel something unlock. Itsy Bitsy was wrong. I knew this all along. I could not see Itsy Bitsy. I never knew who or what she was, and she did not sound like an opening or a lip.

That night, we named her—my husband, Randy, and I. Just like the frogs. Dressed her in sparkles and sexy clothes, put her in front of the body chapel, lit candles. At first we whispered it, "Vulva, vulva," softly to see if she'd hear. "Vulva, vulva, are you there?" There was sweetness and something definitely stirred. "Vulva, vulva, are you real?"

And we sang the vulva song, which didn't involve croaking but kissing, and we danced the vulva dance, which didn't involve hopping but leaping, and all the other body parts were lined up—Betty and Gladys and Shorty—and they were definitely listening.

VAGINA FACT

In some places, Africans seem to have been quietly putting an end to the tradition of genital cutting. In Guinea, for instance, Aja Tounkara Diallo Fatimata, the chief "cutter" in the capital, Conakry, used to be reviled by Western human-rights groups. Then a few years ago, she confessed that she had never actually cut anybody. "I'd just cinch their clitorises to make them scream," she

said, "and tightly bandage them up so that they
walked as though they were in pain."

—from the Center for Reproductive Law and Policy

"What does a vagina smell like?"

Earth.

Wet garbage.

God.

Water.

A brand-new morning.

Depth.

Sweet ginger.

Sweat.

Depends.

Musk.

Me.

No smell, I've been told.

Pineapple.

Chalice essence.

Paloma Picasso.

Earthy meat and musk.

Cinnamon and cloves.

Roses.

Spicy musky jasmine forest, deep, deep forest.

Damp moss.

Yummy candy.

The South Pacific.

Somewhere between fish and lilacs.

Peaches.

The woods.

Ripe fruit.

Strawberry-kiwi tea.

Fish.

Heaven.

Vinegar and water.

Light, sweet liquor.

Cheese.

Ocean.

Sexy.

A sponge.

The beginning.

I have been traveling with this piece all over America (and now, the world) for years. I am threatening to create a vagina-friendly map of all the vagina-friendly cities I have visited. There are many now. There have been many surprises; Oklahoma City surprised me. They were wild for vaginas in Oklahoma City. Pittsburgh surprised me. They love vaginas in Pittsburgh. I have already been there three times. Wherever I go, women come up to me after the show to tell me their sto-

*ries, to make suggestions, to communicate their re-
sponses. This is my favorite part of traveling with the
work. I get to hear the truly amazing stories. They are
told so simply, so matter-of-factly. I am always reminded how extraordinary women's lives are, and how
profound. And I am reminded how isolated women are,
and how oppressed they often become in their isolation.
How few people they have ever told of their suffering and
confusion. How much shame there is surrounding all
this. How crucial it is for women to tell their stories, to
share them with other people, how our survival as
women depends on this dialogue.*

*It was after performing the piece one night in New
York City that I heard the story of a young Vietnamese
woman who, when she was five years old—recently arrived in America, unable to speak English—fell on a fire
hydrant while playing with her best friend, and cut her
vagina. Unable to communicate what had occurred, she
simply hid her bloodied underpants under her bed. Her
mother found them and assumed she'd been raped. As
the young girl did not know the word for "fire hydrant,"
she could not explain to her parents what had really*

happened. Her parents accused her best friend's brother of raping her. They rushed the young girl to the hospital, and a whole group of men stood around her bed, staring at her open, exposed vagina. Then, on the way home, she realized her father was no longer looking at her. In his eyes she had become a used, finished woman. He never really looked at her again.

Or the story of the stunning young woman in Oklahoma, who approached me after the show with her stepmother to tell me how she had been born without a vagina, and only realized it when she was fourteen. She was playing with her girlfriend. They compared their genitals and she realized hers were different, something was wrong. She went to the gynecologist with her father, the parent she was close to, and the doctor discovered that in fact she did not have a vagina or a uterus. Her father was heartbroken, trying to repress his tears and sadness so his daughter would not feel bad. On the way home from the doctor, in a noble attempt to comfort her, he said, "Don't worry, darlin'. This is all gonna be just fine. As a matter of fact, it's gonna be great. We're gonna get you the best homemade pussy in America.

And when you meet your husband, he's gonna know we had it made specially for him." And they did get her a new pussy, and she was relaxed and happy and when she brought her father back two nights later, the love between them melted me.

Then there was the night in Pittsburgh when a woman filled with passion rushed up to tell me she had to speak to me as soon as possible. Her intensity convinced me, and I called her as soon as I got back to New York. She said she was a massage therapist and she had to talk to me about the texture of the vagina. The texture was crucial. I hadn't gotten the texture, she said. And she talked to me for an hour with such detail, with such sensuous clarity, that when she was finished, I had to lie down. During that conversation she also talked to me about the word "cunt." I had said something negative about it in my performance, and she said I didn't understand the word at all. She needed to help me reconceive it. She talked to me for a half-hour more about the word "cunt" and when she was finished, I was a convert. I wrote this for her.

RECLAIMING CUNT

I call it cunt. I've reclaimed it, "cunt." I really like it. "Cunt." Listen to it. "Cunt." C C, Ca Ca. Cavern, cackle, clit, cute, come—closed c—closed inside, inside ca—then u—then cu—then curvy, inviting sharkskin u—uniform, under, up, urge, ugh, ugh, u—then n then cun—snug letters fitting perfectly together—n—nest, now, nexus, nice, nice, always depth, always round in uppercase, cun, cun—n a jagged wicked electrical pulse—

n [high-pitched noise] then soft n—warm n—cun, cun, then t—then sharp certain tangy t—texture, take, tent, tight, tantalizing, tensing, taste, tendrils, time, tactile, tell me, tell me "Cunt cunt," say it, tell me "Cunt." "Cunt."

"*If your vagina got dressed, what would it wear?*"

"Red high-tops and a Mets cap worn back-
ward."

"*If it could speak, what would it say?*"

"It would say words that begin with 'V' and
'T'—'turtle' and 'violin' are examples."

"What does your vagina remind you of?"

"A pretty dark peach. Or a diamond I found from a treasure and it's mine."

"What's special about your vagina?"

"Somewhere deep inside it I know it has a really really smart brain."

"What does your vagina smell like?"

"Snowflakes."

THE WOMAN
WHO LOVED TO MAKE
VAGINAS HAPPY

I love vaginas. I love women. I do not see them as separate things. Women pay me to dominate them, to excite them, to make them come. I did not start out like this. No, to the contrary: I started out as a lawyer. But in my late thirties, I became obsessed with making women happy. There were so many unfulfilled women. So many women who had no access to their sexual happiness. It began as a mission of sorts, but then I got involved in it. I got very good at it, kind of brilliant. It was my art. I started getting paid for it. It was as if I had found my calling. Tax law seemed completely boring and insignificant then.

I wore outrageous outfits when I dominated women—lace and silk and leather—and I used props: whips, handcuffs, rope, dildos. There was nothing like this in tax law. There were no props, no excitement, and I hated those blue corporate suits, although I wear them now from time to time in my new line of work and they serve quite nicely. Context is all. There were no props, no outfits in corporate law. There was no wetness. There was no dark mysterious foreplay. There were no erect nipples. There were no delicious mouths, but mainly there was no moaning. Not the kind I'm talking about, anyway. This was the key, I see now; moaning was the thing that ultimately seduced me and got me addicted to making women happy. When I was a little girl and I would see women in the movies making love, making strange orgasmic moaning noises, I used to laugh.

I got strangely hysterical. I couldn't believe that big, outrageous, ungoverned sounds like that just came out of women.

I longed to moan. I practiced in front of my mirror, on a tape recorder, moaning in various keys, various tones, with sometimes very operatic expressions, sometimes with more reserved, almost withheld expression. But always when I played it back, it sounded fake. It *was* fake. It wasn't rooted in anything sexual, really, only in my desire to be sexual.

But then when I was ten I had to pee really badly once. On a car trip. It went on for almost an hour and when I finally got to pee in this dirty little gas station, it was so exciting, I moaned. I moaned as I peed. I couldn't believe it, me moaning in a Texaco station somewhere in the middle of Louisiana. I realized right then that moans are connected with not getting what you want right away, with putting things off. I realized moans were best when they caught you by surprise; they came out of this hidden mysteri-

ous part of you that was speaking its own language. I realized that moans were, in fact, that
language.

I became a moaner. It made most men anx-
ious. Frankly, it terrified them. I was loud and
they couldn't concentrate on what they were
doing. They'd lose focus. Then they'd lose everything. We couldn't make love in people's homes.
The walls were too thin. I got a reputation in my
building, and people stared at me with contempt
in the elevator. Men thought I was too intense;
some called me insane.

I began to feel bad about moaning. I got
quiet and polite. I made noise into a pillow. I
learned to choke my moan, hold it back like a
sneeze. I began to get headaches and stress-
related disorders. I was becoming hopeless when I
discovered women. I discovered that most women
loved my moaning—but, more important, I discovered how deeply excited I got when other
women moaned, when I could make other women
moan. It became a kind of passion.

Discovering the key, unlocking the vagina's mouth, unlocking this voice, this wild song.

I made love to quiet women and I found this place inside them and they shocked themselves in their moaning. I made love to moaners and they found a deeper, more penetrating moan. I became obsessed. I longed to make women moan, to be in charge, like a conductor, maybe, or a band-leader.

It was a kind of surgery, a kind of delicate science, finding the tempo, the exact location or home of the moan. That's what I called it.

Sometimes I found it over a woman's jeans. Sometimes I sneaked up on it, off the record, quietly disarming the surrounding alarms and moving in. Sometimes I used force, but not violent, oppressing force, more like dominating, "I'm going to take you someplace; don't worry, lie back, enjoy the ride" kind of force. Sometimes it was simply mundane. I found the moan before things even started, while we were eating salad or chicken just casually right there, with my fingers,

"Here it is like that," real simple, in the kitchen, all mixed in with the balsamic vinegar. Sometimes I used props—I loved props—sometimes I made the woman find her own moan in front of me. I waited, stuck it out until she opened herself. I wasn't fooled by the minor, more obvious moans. No, I pushed her further, all the way into her power moan.

There's the clit moan (a soft, in-the-mouth sound), the vaginal moan (a deep, in-the-throat sound), the combo clit-vaginal moan. There's the pre-moan (a hint of sound), the almost moan (a circling sound), the right-on-it moan (a deeper, definite sound), the elegant moan (a sophisticated laughing sound), the Grace Slick moan (a rock-singing sound), the WASP moan (no sound), the semireligious moan (a Muslim chanting sound), the mountaintop moan (a yodeling sound), the baby moan (a googie-googie-googie-goo sound), the doggy moan (a panting sound), the southern moan (southern accent—"yeah! yeah"), the uninhibited militant bisexual moan (a deep, aggressive, pounding sound), the machine-gun moan, the tortured Zen moan (a twisted, hungry sound), the diva moan (a high, operatic note), the twisted-toe-orgasm moan, and, finally, the surprise triple orgasm moan.

After I finished this piece I read it to the woman on whose interview I'd based it. She didn't feel it really had anything to do with her. She loved the piece, mind you, but she didn't see herself in it. She felt that I had some-how avoided talking about vaginas, that I was still somehow objectifying them. Even the moans were a way of objectifying the vagina, cutting it off from the rest of the vagina, the rest of the woman. There was a real dif-

ference in the way lesbians saw vaginas. I hadn't yet captured it.

So I interviewed her again.

"As a lesbian," she said, "I need you to start from a lesbian-centered place, not framed within a heterosexual context. I did not desire women, for example, because I disliked men. Men weren't even part of the equation."
She said, "You need to talk about entering into vaginas. You can't talk about lesbian sex without doing this.

"For example," she said. "I'm having sex with a woman. She's inside me. I'm inside me. Fucking myself together with her. There are four fingers inside me; two are hers, two are mine."

I don't know that I wanted to talk about sex. But then again, how can I talk about vaginas without talking about them in action? I am worried about the titillation factor, worried about the piece becoming exploitative. Am I talking about vaginas to arouse people? Is that a bad thing?

"As lesbians," she said, "we know about vaginas. We touch them. We lick them. We play with them. We tease them. We notice when the clitoris swells. We notice our own."

I realize I am embarrassed, listening to her. There is a combination of reasons: excitement, fear, her love of vaginas and comfort with them and my distancing, terror of saying all this in front of you, the audience.

"I like to play with the rim of the vagina," she said, "with fingers, knuckles, toes, tongue. I like to enter it slowly, slowly entering, then thrusting three fingers inside.

"There's other cavities, other openings; there's the mouth. While I have a free hand, there's fingers in her mouth, fingers in her vagina, both going, all going all at

once, her mouth sucking my fingers, her vagina sucking my fingers. Both sucking, both wet."

I realize I don't know what is appropriate. I don't even know what that word means. Who decides. I learn so much from what she's telling me. About her, about me.

"Then I come to my own wetness," she says. "She can enter me. I can experience my own wetness, let her slide her fingers into me, her fingers into my mouth, my vagina, the same. I pull her hand out of my cunt. I rub my wetness against her knee so she knows. I slide my wetness down her leg until my face is between her thighs."

Does talking about vaginas ruin the mystery, or is that just another myth that keeps vaginas in the dark, keeps them unknowing and unsatisfied?

"My tongue is on her clitoris. My tongue replaces my fingers. My mouth enters her vagina."

Saying these words feels naughty, dangerous, too direct, too specific, wrong, intense, in charge, alive.

"My tongue is on her clitoris. My tongue replaces my fingers. My mouth enters her vagina."

To love women, to love our vaginas, to know them and touch them and be familiar with who we are and what we need. To satisfy ourselves, to teach our lovers to satisfy us, to be present in our vaginas, to speak of them out loud, to speak of their hunger and pain and loneliness and humor, to make them visible so they cannot be ravaged in the dark without great consequence, so that our center, our point, our motor, our dream, is no longer detached, mutilated, numb, broken, invisible, or ashamed.

"You have to talk about entering vaginas," she said. "Come on," I say, "come in."

I had been performing this piece for over two years when it suddenly occurred to me that there were no pieces about birth. It was a bizarre omission. Although when I told a journalist this recently, he asked me, "What's the connection?"

Almost twenty-one years ago I adopted a son, Dylan, who was very close in age to me. Last year he and his wife, Shiva, had a baby. They asked me to be present for the birth. I don't think, in all my investiga-

tion, that I really understood vaginas until this mo-ment. If I was in awe of them before the birth of my granddaughter, Colette, I am certainly in deep worship now.

I WAS THERE IN
THE ROOM

For Shiva

I was there when her vagina opened.
We were all there: her mother, her husband,
    and I,
and the nurse from the Ukraine with her
    whole hand
up there in her vagina feeling and turning with
    her rubber
glove as she talked casually to us—like she was
    turning on a loaded faucet.

I was there in the room when the contractions
made her crawl on all fours,
made unfamiliar moans leak out of her pores
and still there after hours when she just
      screamed suddenly
wild, her arms striking at the electric air.

I was there when her vagina changed
from a shy sexual hole
to an archaeological tunnel, a sacred vessel,
a Venetian canal, a deep well with a tiny stuck
      child inside,
waiting to be rescued.

I saw the colors of her vagina. They changed.
Saw the bruised broken blue
the blistering tomato red
the gray pink, the dark;
saw the blood like perspiration along the edges
saw the yellow, white liquid, the shit, the clots
pushing out all the holes, pushing harder and
      harder,

saw through the hole, the baby's head
scratches of black hair, saw it just there behind
the bone—a hard round memory,
as the nurse from the Ukraine kept turning and
        turning
her slippery hand.

I was there when each of us, her mother and I,
held a leg and spread her wide pushing
with all our strength against her pushing
and her husband sternly counting, "One, two,
        three,"
telling her to focus, harder.
We looked into her then.
We couldn't get our eyes out of that place.

We forget the vagina, all of us
what else would explain
our lack of awe, our lack of wonder.

I was there when the doctor
reached in with Alice in Wonderland spoons

and there as her vagina became a wide operatic
    mouth
singing with all its strength;
first the little head, then the gray flopping arm,
    then the fast
swimming body, swimming quickly into our
    weeping arms.

I was there later when I just turned and faced
    her vagina.
I stood and let myself see
her all spread, completely exposed
mutilated, swollen, and torn,
bleeding all over the doctor's hands
who was calmly sewing her there.

I stood, and as I stared, her vagina suddenly
became a wide red pulsing heart.

The heart is capable of sacrifice.
So is the vagina.
The heart is able to forgive and repair.

It can change its shape to let us in.

It can expand to let us out.

So can the vagina.

It can ache for us and stretch for us, die for us

and bleed and bleed us into this difficult,

wondrous world.

So can the vagina.

I was there in the room.

I remember.

V - DAY

THE STORY OF V-DAY AND THE COLLEGE INITIATIVE

by Karen Obel, Director, V-Day College Initiative

I didn't find V-Day. It found me.

I had been on the board of directors of the Feminist.com website for just over a year when I went to a board meeting to which Eve Ensler had been invited at the suggestion of Kathy Najimy. Kathy thought some of our goals at Feminist.com overlapped with Eve's goal to stop violence against women. Kathy was right: By the end of the meeting, V-Day was conceived.

The V-Day Benefit Committee was made up of women whom each of us invited to join and still others whom they invited and so on. Our first project was V-Day 1998, the event that was to launch the V-Day movement and the first of many events to raise money and awareness to stop violence against women. V-Day 1998 was a celebrity benefit performance of Eve's play *The Vagina Monologues* at New York City's Hammerstein Ballroom Theatre. The performance had sold out, but outside on the street, hundreds of people still clamored to get in. Everyone wanted to be a part of V-Day, the groundbreaking event that forever changed the meaning of Valentine's Day.

For me, the tone was set by Glenn Close during rehearsals the day before the performance. I was in the box office when I heard her ask Eve for direction on the subtleties of pronunciation in her particular monologue.

"Is it ehr, ehr, ehr or ahr, ahr, ahr?" she asked.

Out of context, the question might seem pedestrian, even silly. But hearing Glenn and watching her prepare, I became acutely aware of how profoundly committed the V-Day 1998 participants were to the event and how clearly they understood the importance of the messages of *The Vagina Monologues* and the V-Day movement. And the audience got it too. The men and women, students and businesspeople, mothers and activists in the theater—alternately laughing, gasping, silent, crying, and cheering—received the performances with open arms, hearts, and minds. By the time Glenn Close reached the climax of "Reclaiming Cunt," she had worked the audience into such a frenzy that when she demanded their response, they could not keep themselves from answering.

Despite the resistance of potential sponsors and advertisers to V-Day 1998—for some reason, a lot of people have trouble with the word *vagina*—the event was a huge critical and financial success. *The New York Times,* which initially would not run a paid-for ad for the event because it considered the logo too suggestive, eventually accepted an altered version, and ended up reviewing the event as "the hottest ticket in town."

Much hard work and dedication were required of the Benefit Committee to make that first V-Day the success that it was. Our responsibilities grew dramatically as the demands on us increased. I started as a "regular" volunteer, was made the committee's secretary, and became coordinating producer by curtain time. During the year in which we worked to make it happen, I would often ask myself why I was giving so much to V-Day, an organization working to stop violence against women, worthy though the cause was. After all, I am fortunate never to have been a victim of violence. Yet in the months leading up to the event, I would come home every day from my more-than-full-time job and spend three to ten hours answering e-mail, drafting and sending letters and other documents, creating seating plans and invitations, and so much more. I was tired *all the time,* but I couldn't have been happier or more inspired. I floated through my days joyfully and with a strong sense of purpose.

On the night of the show, I sat in the audience among friends and family, my mother next to me. At the end of the performance, Eve came out on the stage and asked those of us who were or knew victims of violence to stand. I stood. My mother stood. Almost everyone in the audience stood. I began to understand "Why V-Day?"

A few weeks later, the V-Day Benefit Committee met to revel in the success of the evening and to discuss what we could do better next time. For the first time in a year, we didn't have an imminent event to focus on. For the first time in a year, I heard the women I had come to know as strong, brilliant, creative, and self-sufficient, and whom I thought I knew so well, tell stories about violence in their own lives that stunned me. These women had been so selflessly dedicated to mounting the production that, during a year of endless meetings, not once did they allow us to stray from our purpose by calling attention to themselves. When they finally spoke, they shared experiences of abuse so horrific that I wouldn't have believed them if I hadn't heard them with my own ears.

When I left that meeting I was numb, but again I knew "Why V-Day?" I realized that many people I knew and would come to know have had similar experiences of abuse, similar stories to those I had heard that night. I decided I would do whatever I could to change the world so as to eliminate the causes and sources of violence against women, to prevent their devastating effects.

Since the first step to eradicating a societal problem is making people aware that it exists, the V-Day Benefit Committee decided that the goal for 1999 would be to get our message out at the local level. We came up with the idea for the V-Day College Initiative. We would invite colleges and universities to mount productions of *The Vagina Monologues* on Valentine's Day, the proceeds from which would go back into their communities through organizations working to stop violence against women. I volunteered to direct the project.

I had high hopes for the College Initiative, although I had no idea what to expect, how it would be received, or what it could realistically achieve. I began by going on-line to research colleges and universities in the United States. I spent countless hours each day for weeks sending letters to women's studies and theater

departments, professors, student activities organizations, health educators, campus theater groups—to
any person I thought would be likely to read my letters
and respond—at every school on my various lists until
the pictures and words on my computer screen started
to blur. If people did respond, they were sometimes cu-
rious, sometimes suspicious, sometimes hostile, and
sometimes enthusiastic. Some had heard of *The Vagina
Monologues,* although it wasn't as well known then as it
is now. Many were interested in the idea of the College
Initiative but couldn't believe that it could be so ac-
cessible and straightforward, that there was no cost to
participate and no hidden agenda.

As things started taking shape, my contacts kept
me posted on their progress. Sometimes they expressed
concern about the small number of people showing up
for auditions, the difficulty in getting people to attend
their productions, and the criticism and backlash from
those who didn't see the merit in what they were doing
or were outright opposed to it. Occasionally, they
would ask to withdraw from the Initiative—because resistance at their schools became too strong, because
they didn't believe they had the support or resources to
mount the kind of event they envisioned, or because
they found they were neglecting their personal responsibilities. In these instances I was back to square one,
but with much less time to find replacements. Some-

times I was able to convince people to persevere. This was the case with the folks at my own alma mater, Cornell University: They stuck it out, ended up participating for two years in a row, and have had successful events and tremendously rewarding experiences. Like the Cornell team, those who made it all the way through wrote excitedly of sponsors coming out of the woodwork, favorable local press, the sheer joy and power they felt from being part of the V-Day community, and their astonishment at their own ability to pull off their events.

In the end, my targeted letters, the V-Day website, www.vday.org, and word-of-mouth worked to bring more than sixty-five schools in the United States and Canada to the V-Day 1999 College Initiative. I was initially disappointed in the final total, but then I realized how significant it was to have gotten any schools at all to participate. More important, I thought of the devotion of those who took part, and came to consider the College Initiative no less than a monumental achievement for V-Day. Our activities were covered extensively in the media, and they introduced more than 20,000 people in North America to V-Day and *The Vagina Monologues.* During the week following Valentine's Day, I received an extraordinary number of inquiries from my contacts asking when they could start to work on the following year's program:

We found out about V-Day just about four weeks ago but were able to pull together a performance in that short time. Our drama department wasn't interested in participating, so we recruited anyone who wanted to read: We had professors, a few women from the surrounding community, sculpture majors, women's studies majors, law students. I have to say I am truly in awe of these women. They all did an absolutely wonderful job. We were laughing and crying, some gave me goosebumps listening to them. We had just under 200 people show up and every one of them was blown away. I don't think they knew what to expect but after the show there were so many people coming up to me saying they wished they had brought this person or that person, that more people needed to hear the message.

I just can't say enough. We've received so much positive feedback already. We had a really diverse audience and they were so receptive and supportive, it was just a great feeling all around, and I'm sad it's over! But we all can't wait until next year! I need to sleep for about a week, then I'm ready to start planning again! Karen, just say the word!

—Michele, Northern Illinois
University College of Law, February 19, 1999

We realized we would have to do another year of the College Initiative. So we did. Three things distinguished the V-Day 2000 College Initiative from its predecessor: sponsors, the Empowerment Workshop, and worldwide penetration.

After sponsoring a small but significant event in 1999, the basis for a layout in its February issue, *Self* magazine decided to sponsor the *entire* 2000 Initiative. Planned Parenthood Federation of America came on board as the primary sponsor of the 2000 Initiative's special event—the Empowerment Workshop. On November 6, 1999, students from a hundred of the participating schools came to New York to attend a workshop led by Eve. Eve taught the students how to mount a production of *The Vagina Monologues* at their schools, and then they went to see her perform the play at the Westside Theatre. Students spent the weekend immersed in V-Day events, cultivating friendships with their fellow College Initiative participants. In feedback after their local V-Day events, many who had come to New York highlighted the Empowerment Workshop as one of their favorite Initiative experiences.

While the V-Day 1999 College Initiative participants were from the United States and Canada, some of the participants in 2000 came from other parts of the world, considerably expanding V-Day's reach. One hundred and fifty schools joined us, from San Francisco State University in California and Cornish College of the Arts in Washington State to Oxford University in England and Friedrich Schiller Universität in Germany. Based on figures reported by the participating schools, it is estimated that about 65,000 people attended V-Day 2000 College Initiative events and that, through these events and the associated publicity, more than 15 million people were introduced to *The Vagina Monologues* and V-Day around the world. When the figures from both College Initiatives are added to those of people who have celebrated V-Day through celebrity benefit performances of *The Vagina Monologues* worldwide, the total number of people who have been touched by V-Day in the three years since its launch is simply unimaginable.

Once again, Initiative participants clamored for a repeat performance. So I will be directing the program for the third year in 2001.

While most of the people who volunteer to coordinate the College Initiative at their schools are college-age women, there are also some men, some professors, some campus theater directors. Some are feminists and some are just regular folks with no previously embraced causes. For various reasons, all see the merit of bringing V-Day to their communities. And despite the fact that all participating schools mount performances of the same piece—*The Vagina Monologues*—each event is unique. Some are intimate staged readings. Others are extravagant theatrical and social happenings. Many schools offer additional activities, information, and resources in conjunction with their events. There are "Vagina Dialogues" following performances. There are sexual-assault counselors on site. There are fund-raisers and parties. There is music and art and dance.

Arizona State University constructed a forty-foot inflatable vagina to surround the entrance of its venue; the Rochester Institute of Technology did its production simultaneously in English and American Sign Language; Washington University in St. Louis displayed the Clothesline Project in conjunction with its event (the Clothesline Project, started in Hyannis, Massachusetts, in October 1990, works to stop violence against women by encouraging women who have experienced abuse to tell their stories on T-shirts that are then hung on a clothesline—society's dirty laundry for all to see); a "Feminist InfoFest" ran alongside Middlebury's performance; the University of Nebraska, Lincoln, offered a raffle (with prizes from local restaurants, massage wellness clinics and salons, artwork donated by local artists, and a free annual exam from its local chapter of Planned Parenthood) and an information/activist booth sponsored by the Women's Studies Association in the student union; the University of Nevada, Las Vegas, had a "V-Day Wall" set piece—a collage of the history of V-Day, with images of the cast, words, and valentine hearts.

As these examples illustrate, the College Initiative events are as varied as the people who produce them.

Although the College Initiative was originally conceived to spread the V-Day message to a larger, grassroots audience, three other important outcomes have materialized in the course of the project.

First, for many of the young women and men who choose to participate, it is one of the biggest and most demanding projects they have ever undertaken. There are basic challenges, such as securing a venue for the production, locating funding and sponsorship, holding auditions and selecting a cast, assembling a production team, publicizing the event, pursuing press coverage, rehearsing, selecting beneficiary organizations, and presenting the actual event, all the while juggling the daily responsibilities of being a student. Less common but often more difficult challenges have arisen at many of the schools. These ranged from event posters being defaced to actresses and funders pulling out at the last minute to threatened job stability, departmental dismantling and event disruption, and even hostile state legislative action. Arizona State University's V-Day 1999 production of *The Vagina Monologues* was cited by House Appropriations Subcommittee on Education chairperson Linda Gray as one of the reasons she had submitted a proposal to eliminate $1.6 million in funding for the women's studies programs at three Arizona universities. Ms. Gray subsequently withdrew her proposal. At Washington University in St. Louis during the 2000 Initiative, a group of fraternity members posted antagonistic flyers and threatened to disrupt the V-Day event. But the student director turned an intimidating and potentially destructive situation into a positive and constructive one: She invited the men to her production, where they watched in rapt attention. Apologizing to her after the show, they confessed that they hadn't realized the severity of the problem of violence against women.

Like this student, many participants were triumphant in the face of adversity. Despite (or perhaps because of) how demanding College Initiative events can be, the extent to which so many people—particularly young women—become empowered by successfully developing and executing their productions is staggering. Many people never have the opportunity, desire, or ability to tackle in a lifetime what (mostly) seventeen- to twenty-one-year-old women achieve in a semester.

Dear Karen,

On a personal level, the College Initiative will be the experience that I remember most from my college career. Directing The Vagina Monologues *taught me more about myself than anything I have ever done. It also reinforced my belief in the power of community, especially a strong community of women. To sit in the audience, watching my once-shy actresses laugh and moan and cry about their vaginas, and feel the power that their words had over the people surrounding me was indescribable.*

—Danielle, Colorado State University,
May 19, 2000

As Danielle's letter expresses, many of the young women and men who participate in the College Initiative experience a heightened awareness of "the power of community, especially a strong community of women" and the need for such a community. This is the second magnificent, unanticipated outcome of the College Initiative: *The Vagina Monologues* and V-Day are helping to bring a new generation to a new kind of feminism.

Finally, and perhaps most important, many of the people who have come into the fold in various capacities (as contacts, actresses, helpers, or audience members) have done so with a conscious or sometimes subconscious desire to heal from personal experiences of sexual violation. Many of them have written to me of their feelings of isolation, fear, helplessness, despair, pain, and lack of self-worth, and their belief that they would never recover from their abusive experiences—until they found *The Vagina Monologues* and V-Day. The play and the movement have served as vehicles for their present recovery and future survival.

Karen, I just had to respond to your e-mail and let you know that meeting you and Eve has been one of the most special and important experiences in my life to date. You give me some indication of the woman I want to be.

I know I did not discuss this with you before, it's not some-
thing I discuss often, but I have been sexually abused.

This V-Day experience—being a part of this wonderful
project, meeting women who have made it to adulthood as
strong, intelligent, together, interesting, as well as interacting
with peers of mine who have given thought to the same issues
I have and are willing to work to prevent what happened to
myself and countless other young women from happening
again—has reminded me what I lost in my rush to recover: I
lost my body and now I know I will get it back.

With energy,

—Anonymous student, October 21, 1998

Directing the V-Day College Initiative has been
much more demanding and rewarding than I ever expected it to be. For two years, I have received twenty-five
to seventy-five e-mails a day regarding the Initiative. I
have responded to all of them. And that has been only a
fraction of my daily responsibilities. I have never given
myself more fully to any project in my life. There have
been days when I would be in my twelfth exhausting
hour at the computer and I would ask myself again,
"Why V-Day?" and then I'd get a letter from one of the
Initiative participants and, again, the answer was clear.

Some of these letters follow, but there are hundreds more like them from people all over the world of
all backgrounds and ethnicities who have found,

through *The Vagina Monologues* and V-Day, new ways of thinking and talking about their concerns, discovering their own potential, helping others, healing themselves. I am certain, when you read these letters, that you'll know "Why V-Day?" too.

LETTERS AND STORIES

The Beginning

I feel (who doesn't?) that V-Day is a very important cause, and I think it's a good strategy as well. It gets people who ordinarily wouldn't even think about women's issues to come to the play and most of them leave with a new understanding and a lot more respect for the experiences of women in our society. It's also empowering for the people involved, both to have the experience of using their voice to say (to 400+ people) something so meaningful and powerful, and to take active steps to make the world better, safer, and more respectful for women.

—Brian, University of Oklahoma

[To her fellow College Initiative participants]

I want you to not worry. We did this last year and are doing it again, with 8 directors, a 150-person team and 10 other V-Day-related activities (including a concert, an art show, a vulva puppet-making workshop, a zine, a lecture series and more). It is SOOO insane and hard to manage. We won't have tryouts until November 30. We don't have funding. So, while we may LOOK organized, things are ALWAYS insane. Every group does it by its own rules. Don't sweat it if your approach is different. There are pluses and minuses to each. Find what works for you. There is no ONE WAY to do this. Don't stress, just enjoy it—it will work out. <GRIN> good luck!

—Danah, Brown University

[To her fellow College Initiative participants]

We had auditions before Thanksgiving break and some 40 women tried out, which was spectacular. We ended up casting nine and were fairly successful in reaching out to a diverse group of women as far as ethnicity, race, sexuality, age, whatever. Rehearsals have already begun and I'm so excited. As far as sponsors—all of our money is coming from on-campus groups. We are lucky enough to have an on-campus arts grant that provides easy-to-get funding for plays/concerts/etc. but I am in the process of finding funding for the other more political projects we are doing. For that money I have approached our Women's Studies Department and am planning to approach American Studies, Sociology, African-American Studies (one of our speakers is talking about poor minority women), and any other academic department that might be considered relevant. I am also presenting a proposed budget to our on-campus community service umbrella, which will provide a couple hundred dollars for one-time projects. If you are at a university, pull from the grad schools—I am planning to approach the feminist law journal at the law school for money and for other types of support and will be checking to see if the other grad schools here have women's groups with available funds. And, if you have a fairly liberal college, try the administration—we are approaching the Dean of Students who has a discretionary fund (although that's a little bit of a stretch). For those of you with less on-campus funding sources, if you are involving non-student communities, see if you can get money from a local community loan fund or the education department of your local/state Planned Parenthood. Even if they can't give you money, they may be able to refer you to someone who can. Hope that helps!

—Anika, Yale University

I would just like to say that bringing *The Vagina Monologues* and the V-Day celebration to Lincoln, Nebraska, is a HUGE deal. Lincoln is an ultra-conservative town that when viewed from the outside would appear to care nothing about "women's issues." Nebraska is famous for its "Husker Mania" where during college football season most people go to "church" twice a week, once on Saturday afternoon, and once on the usual Sunday morning. This is a state where a retired football coach/demigod is running for the U.S. Senate position, and has a pretty darned good chance at winning. This is a state where violence against women is normalized. Just a few short years ago, a certain favorite football star was given a slap on the wrist and sent back out on the field after missing only a few games, for beating up his estranged girlfriend. Coincidentally, I believe the Huskers brought home the national title that year.

In spite of the apathetic position of our notorious athletic department, there are many passionate individuals in this community who are dedicated to stopping the violence. I am overwhelmed by the overall positive response that I have gotten for bringing this show to Lincoln. It will truly open some eyes, minds, and hearts!

—Keri, University of Nebraska, Lincoln

The Buildup

In this environment, *The Vagina Monologues* was not initially well received. Now, support has come forth from various departments on campus with donations. I have booked one performance at a 450-person venue. Now I am not so sure that 450 seats will be enough.

—David, Oregon State University

I'm trying to work in the community. I've contacted several shelters and programs, and they're very interested. They ask me, OK, what do you want us to do? This is where I choke up.

—Laura, University of Puget Sound

I just wanted to thank you once again for giving Colorado State University permission to do *The Vagina Monologues* last November. Our show was a huge success and "vagina" is still the hottest buzzword on our campus. We completely sold out our run in an 80-seat theatre, and had to add two shows and break fire code (Shhh!) by squeezing in 20 extra seats each night. We cleared over $1,000 for the Crossroads Safehouse in Fort Collins. Because we were able to direct the show earlier, I am also able to revive it for Valentine's Day. This time, we are doing two shows that night in a 650-seat theatre and publicity has been donated by organizations all over our once-conservative little town. This show has done so much for all of us, and I just wanted you to know that by stretching the rules for us, our message reached hundreds of people.

—Danielle, Colorado State University

We have been posting little teasers every week to let people know that the show is coming, things like " 'What are we saying about our bodies if we can't say vagina?'—Eve Ensler" or "Have you made a clitoris happy today?" or "V-Day is coming . . ." Well, our teasers keep mysteriously disappearing and one of our cast members noticed one of our flyers that had been defaced (the clitoris one). The word "clitoris" had been scratched out and a penis had been drawn in, and not just any penis, but a penis ejaculating. I've also been hearing people on campus commenting about the show: "Vaginas?! Jesus." (laughter) "What are we saying about our vaginas?!" (laughter)

But I guess that's what this show is for, to dissipate this ignorance.

—Eman, University of California at Santa Cruz

It has been such an exciting and exhilarating experience, I don't know where to begin. Somehow, with hard work and effort and love, it's all coming together. We have some fantastic actresses, undergrads, grads and alumnae, as well as a few non-Columbia actresses. We've been rehearsing like crazy, and I can't tell you what a profound experience it is. I keep learning more and more about *The Vagina Monologues* and about women. It's wonderful.

—Joan, Columbia University

Dear Karen,

I just want to tell you how deeply moved I am by all of the women who have come forward to donate their time to our Women's Resource Center production of *The Vagina Monologues*. I had no idea when I replied to your e-mail that this event would become such a powerful experience for so many of us. I worry a little about negative backlash from certain individuals at this university but am completely dedicated to this project. So, there is much more in my heart to say but I have so much to do in running the Women's Resource Center, including making time to memorize my lines, that I must go for now. Please thank Eve Ensler for what she has given us and you for all your hard organizational work! By the way, we are close to selling out our 300-seat venue. It's amazing!

Another Vagina Warrior,

—Sandrea, University of New Mexico
Women's Resource Center

Karen, approximately 31 faculty, staff, and students will collaborate in performing the show. The entire performance will be presented simultaneously in English and in American Sign Language (approximately 10% of our population is deaf). Staging will be fairly simple—for most monologues two actors will be on stage, one performing in spoken English, the other in ASL. A few of the monologues will be ensemble pieces, including "Wear and Say," "Smell," "My Mother Slapped Me," and "I Was There in the Room." In between the monologues, a slide will be displayed on a large screen with one of the violence statistics given to us in our V-Day packets. Before and after the show, taped music will be played which celebrates women, women's health, women's sexuality, women's empowerment. Before and after the show, there will be informational tables set up from local health agencies, as well as sales of the book, T-shirts, buttons, and vagina chocolates. At the reception, we are making plans to have artwork by a student who does paintings of vaginas.

—Julie, Coordinator of the Women's Center,
Rochester Institute of Technology

Just had to share! Our largest local newspaper is extremely (putting it mildly) conservative and I expected that even though the arts desk is on friendly terms with several cast members, we would be listed in some dark recess of the classified section. I just spoke with our friend and not ONLY will we have a nice-sized article in the Sunday edition, but he was granted permission to actually PRINT "VAGINA" ONE TIME!! Please remember we are talking KNOXVILLE, TENNESSEE, where the grocery stores block the cover photos of *Cosmopolitan* magazine because the images are too suggestive!! We ARE making a difference!! VIVE V-DAY!!!

—Linda, University of Tennessee, Knoxville

I just wanted to thank you and Eve (and all the other people whose names I don't know) for making this possible. Since becoming involved in this project, I have learned to respect myself more. I take more chances. I am just a happier person overall, because I feel that I am a part of something so colossal and important and compelling and breathtaking—the list goes on and on. And, I am proud to say that I now have no problem saying vagina. In fact, I literally say it at least five times a day lately.

Sincerely,

—Jenna, Carnegie Mellon University

The Events

We are already sold out for all of our shows. This is going to be insane. We sold out in a couple of hours!

—Danah, Brown University

We are performing at 3:30 today.

Yesterday's rehearsal was unbelievably emotional. The woman who does "Coochi Snorcher" broke down and sobbed for about five minutes at the line "my coochi snorcher is a very bad place." She was afraid that she won't be able to make it through today's performance without crying. We all said we didn't care if she does cry and probably all the better if she does; people SHOULD be disturbed by that monologue.

Probably the funniest thing about rehearsal yesterday was that we were in the room next to a history conference (on post-colonialism of all things!), and I think they were a little shocked to hear Crista screaming "CUNT, CUNT!! SAY IT! SAY IT! CUNT! CUNT!! SAY IT!! SAY IT!!" and to hear us responding and then when I did the triple surprise orgasm moan . . . well . . . let's just say that they heard that loud and clear too!

—Mary, Michigan State University

[To her fellow College Initiative participants]

I have yet to send out a message into this pool of beautiful vagina-talking women. Better late than never?! I just wanted to say that this is an awesome thing that we are all doing and every time I hear someone ask "Why do a play about vaginas?" I think about all the e-mails I have received and I know that we are taking steps to ensure that maybe for our daughter's granddaughters there won't need to be plays about vaginas, they will be talked about and respected. But until then I remind those people who ask that we have a long bat-

tle in front of us to stop the violation and shame. Happy
V-Day, have a fabulous opening night!

—Amy, University of Washington at Seattle

Directors' Notes

*What, then, are the special ways of women? I have found in
seeking to answer this question a bottomless well of possibility.*

—Shekhinah Mountainwater

From the very beginning, when I waited impatiently
for my Performance Kit to arrive in the mail, my experiences with this play have proven the above quote in-
finitely true. The journey that it has taken me through
has revealed to me the endless possibilities of form,
manner, heart and spirit . . . the things that shape
Woman. Upon reading the script for the first time, I
was struck with the honesty, brilliance and strength of
the women depicted in the monologues. Each had the
ability to evoke genuine, heartfelt emotion through the
stories of their own real lives. The sad ones made me
cry, the comic ones made me laugh . . . most made me
do both at once. These were real women, with real experiences, and each was completely unique . . . a bottomless well of possibility. Time passed, we held
auditions and assembled a company of fairly diverse
women (not one was cut from the show). As we began

to organize ourselves, form plans and rehearse, I grew to know each of the women better and better. Some were actresses from the start, doing the show because it was, in fact, a show. Others were feminists to the core, who had never acted in their lives but wanted to stand up and fight for their own. Most of us were somewhere in between. Those who lived for the stage couldn't help but develop a desire to do their part to end sexual violence. Those who knew nothing of acting often found themselves completely expressing their characters' emotions through the passionate empathy that the script evoked. All of us grew to understand both ends of the spectrum much more deeply than we had before . . . a bottomless well of possibility. So many women, so many spirits, so many stories. . . . It was incredible enough just to experience each person and each story, but I discovered something even closer to home. I discovered the endlessness of what was inside of me. I had pieces of each of these women in my heart, as we all do. I discovered the innate connection we have with each other, the understanding that completely unacquainted women can have of each other. I realized that I can be a director and a feminist and a friend and a student . . . all of these things simply make me a woman. All of us, all women, have this capability to be connected, to be warriors, to be friends, to have as many facets as we wish, to be . . . an endless

well of possibility. Thank you all for joining us today
to celebrate V-Day, enjoy the show!

—Hillary, Michigan State University

What Moved You Most?

Everything went smoothly, people wanted to come,
had to come, needed to come. Wanted more! Chal-
lenged themselves, allowed themselves to feel uncomfortable, really learned something, changed peoples
lives. Watching and listening to the audience, knowing
that I moved them, knowing that they got it. Seeing
my actors grow into women, watching them grow and
change. Watching myself grow and change.

—Laura, California State University,
Long Beach

Working with a fabulous group of women who GAVE
GAVE GAVE! One of my male acting students who attended the performance mentioned afterward that he
never had experienced such SHARING in the theatre
before. He now knew what that word meant. What he
experienced that evening is what I and the other
women who worked on this project had experienced
for the past half year. Working with people who believed in what they were doing, took initiative to make
it happen and followed through with every commit-

ment and more—with good nature and good humor. What more could anyone ask for!?!?!?!

> —Yolanda, University of Detroit, Mercy College, and Oakland Community College

A friend who had told me that she didn't understand why we were doing *The Vagina Monologues* and didn't see the point in always talking about "those things" came to the performance, and the next day told me it had changed her life.

> —Maryann, Carleton College

I love the WORK OF ART on which V-Day is based and I am very passionate about ending sexual violence (all violence really). I must say that if I died tomorrow, after participating in such a wonderful event, I would be able to say that I lived a meaningful life. I of course hope that I don't die tomorrow so that I can continue to be a part of this wondrous movement.

> —Keri, University of Nebraska, Lincoln

Overall, I loved how I felt being part of a movement that empowers women. During the months leading up to the performances, and especially during the few weeks just prior to the event, I relished the fact that I was able to use the word "vagina" in my everyday vocabulary. Every time I saw a cast member on campus, we would speak loudly and confidently about how excited we were to be part of *The VAGINA Monologues.* During staff meetings and in casual conversation with college deans, I would ask if they were going to attend *The VAGINA Monologues.* In dining halls, the campus store, in libraries, bars and restaurants, it was my favorite topic of conversation. Because of the College Initiative, I said VAGINA at least a dozen times a day for two months, and I was able to reclaim it as a word. Thank you, Eve!

—Tyler, Cornell University

I just came back from our event. It was amazing! So many people came that we were turning people away and still, people were squished on the floor and standing outside peeking in for the whole time! I worked with a cast of thirty and we put everything together in two and a half weeks (including auditions!). I was so worried it wouldn't come together but we rocked the house. Major standing ovation!

Thank you so much for doing the amazing work you do to have made this possible. I'm a freshman here and have never directed nor performed and now my life is different, and I was able to bring an amazing piece to so many people. The audience left in a daze. Also, most of my actresses were not "theater people," so that was an amazing element. I don't even know what to say. So I'll just say good night and happy V-Day!

—Cara, Wesleyan University

Hi, Karen. Well, our students did two staged readings over the weekend. The turnout was fabulous on both occasions and the audience loved it. We had lots of male students who attended who were truly moved by it and felt extremely "privileged" to be part of the audience. One guy told me he felt as if he was sitting in a women's locker room listening to the discussion. Another guy asked me to give flowers to all the women but insisted on being anonymous. His card simply read: "To the women of *The Vagina Monologues:* May you always be safe, may you always be strong." Nice, huh!

Many of our women students were blown away by it as well. Our population of students is 45% black and Hispanic. Most are the first to go to college and over 65% of our students come from families with annual incomes of less than $35,000. Generally I have found that our women students haven't been exposed much to feminist literature, thinking, etc. For the most part, political correctness doesn't exist here. So for these women, this was such a powerful experience. One of them said to me afterwards that Eve's book should be a woman's bible!

I also think that this piece is so important for college men. If there's any hope for changing their attitudes and behaviors towards women, letting men experience this play is a good start. That's why this college initiative is so fantastic!

—Toby, Marymount Manhattan College

[To her fellow College Initiative participants]

VAGINA WARRIORS, WOW! I have to tell you all that this has been an amazing experience for us at the University of New Mexico. This letter will be long, so if you're busy you may want to read it later.

This whole project has really changed my life and I want to thank Karen and Eve for that. We started production six weeks ago and Sandrea and I haven't had a day off since. Once we assembled our cast, which included women from the ages of 16 to 60 and was culturally diverse, and got our director, we thought that we were on our way. Since then we have dealt with all manner of crises related to being a woman, including pregnancies and cancer. Two weeks ago our director, an amazing woman, was diagnosed with breast cancer and had to give up the project because of her surgery. (She has now had it and is doing very well.) Sandrea and I took over the direction and I ended up with the part of "Eve." For those of you who were at the [Empowerment Workshop] in New York, I was the one who was too shy to perform in front of everyone and was the curtain for the Spring Preview of Vagina Secret. I had never been on stage before but I knew that I had to do this. I spent the last two weeks memorizing the entire piece.

Then, last Wednesday, a young woman came to the women's center; she had just been raped by two male students. It was 30 minutes before rehearsal but Sandrea and I knew that we had to help her. The story hit the news on Friday and the way in which it was treated by the press infuriated everyone who knew her. Saturday, after rehearsing from 9 to 5, we spent 2½ hours with her and her friends helping them process what had happened. They were all very angry and scared, but the love and support that they showed for one another was amazing! And many women decided to share their own experiences so the young woman would know that she was not alone. It was an incredible experience. The young woman came to our performance last night—she is so brave!

We sold the show out on Friday and turned lots of people away last night; in retrospect we felt that we should have done more than one performance, but who knew? It was a fabulous show! The audience was into it from the introduction. They were so supportive and loving—and they laughed when they were supposed to! Having never done ANY theatre or performance of any kind, I was terrified. Right before the show I sent out a prayer to Eve to be with me and to help me and she did! People told me afterward that they thought I WAS Eve, until I said 21 years ago I adopted a son (and yes, it was very clear in the program that I was playing "Eve"). I was so flattered! We also had six sign language interpreters that were wonderful! They donated their time! Each woman had an interpreter on stage right beside her—it was incredible! People just came out of the woodwork to help us with this project. Oh yeah, we got a standing ovation and three curtain calls!

Thank you so much for all the love and support each of you has shown throughout this project. Good luck to everyone putting up shows this week. Oh, we've made at least $2,200 for the Women's Resource Center and the Albuquerque Rape Crisis Center. VAGINA!

—Summer, University of New Mexico

[To her fellow College Initiative participants]

Congrats to all! It seems we all had a highly successful V-Day! Arizona State University had an overwhelming last-minute response and had to sell standing-room-only tickets at the 4 and 6:30 shows. We did a total of 3 shows on Sunday—a 1:30 free matinee for shelter residents/staff and our sponsors, a 4 P.M. show which raised $1,108, and a 6:30 show which raised $1,209, plus $140 standing-room-only and $75 donation box! The music gala raised $300 and the art show raised I think $500. Our grand total is $3,332!!!!!!! This will be divided in thirds and distributed to AZ Coalition Against Domestic Violence, AZ Sexual Assault Network, and Decolores—the only bilingual domestic violence shelter in AZ!

We had a standing "O" at the 4 P.M. show! It was exhilarating! We did the visual statistic at the beginning of the last opening announcement before the show. ⅓ of the audience stood (every 3rd person given a sticker as they came in the door) to represent that 1 out of every 3 women is raped by the age of 18. It was so in their face and hit them hard! A great way to start the show. People cried!

We also had the Silent Witnesses in the lobby and Project Clothesline. We had T-shirt-making sessions for the Project Clothesline after each show. One woman in her 40's ran to the T-shirt room crying, made a T-shirt that exhibited the fact that she was a survivor of childhood abuse by a family member, passionately sobbing and painting this T-shirt in rage. It took her 10 minutes. When she left, she said, "Thanks!" This is what makes the show worth it. We—all of us—have encouraged women to come share their voices, to not keep them closeted!

I am suffering from great depression right now because I have put so much into this (6 hours a day since September) in addition to being a graduate and post-bac student! I don't want to be JUST a student! I want to do benefit performances for the rest of my life! Is anybody else suffering from this depression of it all being over?

Thank all of you for your inspirational letters and comforting replies. Thank you, Eve and Karen, for giving us this opportunity! It has been incredible!!!!!!!!!!!!!!!!

Love and continual vaginal bliss!

—Amy, Arizona State University

Hello, everyone! I just wanted to wish all of you good luck. If you all have an ounce of the support that V-Day received here at Colorado College, your shows will be HUGE!!! We ended up extending the show to Sunday night. We filled the entire house for the third time (over 200 seats).

A Vagina Story: Saturday night, Megan's mother, grandmother and sisters came to the show. The grandmother is 80 years old. After the show they all went out to dinner. During their meal Megan's grandmother leans over to Megan and says, "Honey, next time I get together with my lady friends, we are going to talk about our vaginas. And if they say WHAT are you talking about? I'm going to say CUNT, CUNT!"

So many stories, so many good memories. We have an enormous, exciting, beautiful and challenging future ahead of us. Good luck to all of you and HAPPY V-DAY!

—Jennifer, Colorado College

WOW. Reading Karen's e-mails was thrilling, I must admit, but being in the *Monologues* themselves was the absolute ideal way to really feel V-Day and what it stands for.

In Blanchard Student Center, we were packed to the hilt—people were sitting on the floor, in the aisles, spewing out from the top of the balcony, cheering and whooping as each monologue was finished.

Everyone was on fire last night. "My Vagina Was My Village" evoked tears and I'm not being facetious. Although all the performers were crying, looking out into the audience, I saw not only women with moist eyes, but men were whipping out the Kleenex and dabbing away.

I don't think I have ever felt the internal pride that I felt last night when I stepped up to the solitary chair in the middle of the stage as the last performer, of "I Was There In the Room." Birth was so beautiful to me, an act that had always been associated with pure pain and torture, that I wanted to give birth on my very own. Though, don't worry, I'm only 18—I have quite a while 'til that happens!! There was a woman in the first row directly in front who cried throughout my piece and during the talk-back asked me if I had ever witnessed a birth and when I answered that I hadn't, she came up to me and hugged me, because she said, "The way you told it to us, that's exactly the way it is." She told me she was an obstetrician, that she had always looked at birth as purely a clinical event, and that now that she thinks about it, each birth is entirely different and beautiful in its own sense.

I am so glad that I had the chance to participate in

The Vagina Monologues this year and I hope I can carry on the tradition for generations to come.

Thank you, Eve, for this amazing opportunity and to every one of you who worked yourself to the bone to make this day across the world happen. Have a Happy V-Day.

—Pia, Mount Holyoke College

Karen! Oh my goddess! Our shows went wonderfully! As you know, the frat boy thing worried me. BUT, we did have one ally in the house. He was the one that was relaying all of my messages to the boys, and he was the one that helped get them to the show. And they came! We reserved the front row for them. Even though only three were responsible for the rude fliers, eight guys showed up! I was stunned! I asked them to wait for me after the show, and they stood in front of me in stunned silence. They apologized with tears in their eyes. They said they had no idea the magnitude and severity of the violence-against-women problem. One of them said (and I quote), "You know I wouldn't have come to this, but I'm very glad I did. This has moved and changed me." Okay, so maybe he wasn't sincere, but I'd like to think that he was. They shook my hand and asked me to apologize to the cast for them. THEN I saw one of them drop a $20 bill in the donation box! It was unreal. There was no protest, no violence, and no heckling. I asked my boyfriend and my three guy friends that were ushering to keep an eye on them. They said that the guys didn't take their eyes off the stage, that they didn't talk during the show, and that they didn't laugh at inappropriate times. Wow! That was only one of the magical stories from last night, but I wanted you to know that it all worked out. Thank you for your words of wisdom (AGAIN!) and all of your advice.

Every woman in the cast has made comments like "This is the most important thing I've ever been a part of" and "I am a different woman because of this." Our director was one of the most talented, inspiring women I've ever worked with, and our cast (19 beautiful, passionate women) was outstanding.

This HAS been the most important thing I've ever done. I am a changed woman. We are wise, VAGINA-talking women and men! What we've done will be remembered. It is important and you have to know that people are going to be more conscious of these issues because of what we've done. I'm proud to BE MY VAGINA.

—Jenn, Washington University, St. Louis

[To her fellow College Initiative participants]

A new term is flying around the UT Knoxville campus—"vagina envy"—everyone wants one! The response was AWESOME to our Monday night show! The audience beat us to our feet to take our bows—

the standing ovation was that intense! What I thought was most incredible was the number of men in the house—they must have been more than ⅓ of the almost 500 people that came. I expected a gigantic gathering of women and to my absolute delight, the guys came out to support vaginas with great respect and gusto! I've been weeping for two days over the e-mail and my knees are weak from the healing power that was spread across the world because of V-Day! Buckets of thanks to everyone! What hit me like a ton of bricks in the afterglow of our awesome evening was—what do I do TODAY to end the violence? I think it's essential that we ride the momentum we have begun. I'm looking into volunteering for our local rape crisis hotline. Any other ideas from you all? Let's keep the movement rollin! VIVE VAGINAS!

—Linda, University of Tennessee, Knoxville

The Vagina Monologues "played Peoria" with a crowd of almost two hundred (which for conservative Bradley University was impressive). It was amazing and awe-inspiring and we almost keeled over when they stood clapping for five minutes.

Today we are all exhausted and proud. How inspiring to spend Valentine's Day on a small quest to save the world. :)

—Vanessa, Bradley University

I don't think my life, or the lives of any of the women who worked on this show, will ever be the same again. I also really enjoyed being connected to the other people around the country/world who were going through many of the same processes as we were. It was very encouraging and helpful to know that there was always a network of very passionate, knowledge-able women and men out there who were willing to listen (see) and respond when there were problems and when there was cause for celebration. I feel as though I have been a part of a truly amazing and pow-erful force. We are on our way to ending the violence that we have endured for far too long! That feels damn good!

—Keri, University of Nebraska, Lincoln

This was a great example of working as a community, not just here in the campus, but within the initiative around the world. The amount of support and accep-tance at a "Lutheran" school has been unreal. Nothing has been censored. My favorite part has been teaching. This message that I have been scrambling to tell the world has reached at least 450 people in a very short amount of time!! A lot of work? Yes. But one man came up to me after the show and said, "Alex, I have learned so much in the past two hours." If that is all I hear about this show forever in my whole life it is

enough. Because he will talk, and tell his friends, and
they will think . . . and just maybe some change will be
made. I do not plan to change the world in a day, but
perhaps in a lifetime, day by day.

—Alex, Pacific Lutheran University

UNTIL THE VIOLENCE STOPS

JOIN THE V-DAY MOVEMENT!

TOGETHER WE CAN STOP THE VIOLENCE!

It is the mission of V-Day to end violence against women by increasing awareness through events and the media and by raising funds to support organizations working to ensure the safety of women everywhere.

V-Day is a movement: an organized effort to finally end violence against women.

V-Day is a vision: we see a civilization where women live in freedom and safety.

V-Day is a spirit: affirming that life should be lived creating and thriving rather than surviving or recovering from terrible atrocities.

V-Day is a catalyst: by raising wide public awareness of the issue, it will reinvigorate efforts already under way and commence new initiatives in publicity, education, and law.

V-Day is a vital ongoing process: we proclaim Valentine's Day as V-Day until the violence against women stops, and then it will become Victory Day.

In just three years, V-Day has raised and donated more

than a million dollars to grassroots organizations that fight violence against women worldwide.

The first V-Day event in 1998 at the Hammerstein Ballroom in New York, featuring Whoopi Goldberg, Glenn Close, Susan Sarandon, and Calista Flockhart, raised $150,000.

In 1999, V-Day at London's Old Vic Theatre, featuring Thandie Newton, Kate Winslet, Kate Blanchette, Gillian Anderson, and Melanie Griffith, gave $275,000 to anti-violence organizations. More than sixty American colleges and universities also had V-Days, raising money and awareness.

In 2000, V-Day was celebrated in Los Angeles, in twelve other cities worldwide, and at 150 colleges. More than $785,000 was given to local, national, and international organizations working to end the violence.

V-Day's Origins and Structure

V-Day was born in 1998 as an outgrowth of *The Vagina Monologues.* As Eve Ensler performed the piece in small towns and large cities all over the world, she saw and heard firsthand the terrible consequences of violence toward women, as hundreds of women told their stories of rape, incest, domestic battery, and genital mutilation. It was clear that something major and dramatic needed to be done. A group of women in New York joined with Eve and founded V-Day . . . a catalyst, a movement, a performance that simply demands that the violence must end.

V-Day is a next-step philanthropy, housed in people's minds and hearts rather than in one physical location. V-Day pays no office rent or other traditional organizational expenses because it is not an organization. V-Day pays only three consultants, and is run almost entirely by volunteers. Eve Ensler has never received payment from V-Day for her work as an author, performer, or organizer. As a result of this nonorganizational form, V-Day is able to give away 85 percent of all funds raised.

Beneficiaries of V-Day Funds

V-Day is proud to be a project of the Tides Center. Tides manages the fiscal and legal areas of V-Day. The Tides Center "strengthens the roots of the social change movement by partnering quality management services with creative programmatic endeavors." A (501)(c)(3) nonprofit public corporation, the Tides Center is a trusted venue for both funders and social entrepreneurs. As an independent organization, the Tides Center provides fiscal sponsorship and core management services to new and innovative nonprofit programs and efforts. Currently, the Tides Center supports more than three hundred projects in forty states and twelve countries.

V-Day distributes the funds collected by donations, ticket sales, advertising, and merchandising to grassroots and field organizations working to stop violence toward women. Funds have been granted to the Anti-Violence Project (N.Y.); Break the Cycle (Los Angeles); Center Against Sexual Abuse (CASA) (Maricopa County, Ariz.); Equality Now (N.Y.); Feminist.com (N.Y.); Haven House (Los Angeles); Human Rights Watch (N.Y., international); Los Angeles Commission on Assaults Against Women (LACAAW); LA Gay and Lesbian Center (Los Angeles); Newham Asian Women's Project (U.K.); New Hope for Women (Belfast, Me.); Planned Parenthood (N.Y., international); Refuge (U.K.); Safe Place and Rape Crisis Center (Sarasota, Fla.); Sanctuary (N.Y.); Santa Fe Rape Crisis Center; Sine (U.K.); Sojourn Services for Battered Women & Their Children

(Los Angeles); Southall Black Sisters (U.K.); The Autonomous Women's House (Zagreb, Croatia); The Revolutionary Association of the Women of Afghanistan (RAWA); Women's AID (U.K.); Women's Commission for Refugee Women and Children and Madre (N.Y.); Women Living Under Muslim Law (France and Algeria).

V-Day 2001 Worldwide Initiative

The V-Day 2001 Worldwide Initiative will support V-Day events in cities and communities around the world during the month of February. These events will use the format that has been so successful in years past. The centerpiece will be a production of Eve Ensler's Obie Award–winning play, *The Vagina Monologues*. Each production will feature women performers both celebrated and less known in the particular region and will raise money to fund organizations working to end violence in those communities.

The Vagina Monologues has had a powerful, often life-changing effect on audiences everywhere, and it is V-Day's plan to go global with a message that entertains and at the same time creates a visceral shift in consciousness. No one who sees the play can remain neutral to the appalling cost of ignoring the global theme of violence against women, its relationship to how we hold human rights, or to the personal cost of such violence. V-Day presents a sweeping movement based on women's ability to speak their truth about violence in a way that liberates rather than condemns, and frees both the spirit and political will. By taking V-Day worldwide, we have the opportunity to use this powerful work as a catalyst for shifting our view of our personal relationship to violence and what is possible in a civil society.

Visit our website at www.vday.org or contact us at <info@vday.org>, 511 Avenue of the Americas, PMB 379, New York, NY 10011-8436.

Every person counts! You can make a difference!

Thank you for adding your power to V-Day.

Willa Shalit
Executive Director

ACKNOWLEDGMENTS

There are so many incredible people who helped give birth to this piece and then sustain it in the world. I want to thank the brave ones who brought it and me to their hometowns and colleges and theaters: Pat Cramer, Sarah Raskin, Gerald Blaise Labida, Howie Baggadonutz, Carole Isenberg, Catherine Gammon, Lynne Hardin, Suzanne Paddock, Robin Hirsh, Gali Gold.

A special thank-you to Steve Tiller and Clive Flowers for a gorgeous British premiere, and to Rada Boric for getting it done with style in Zagreb and for being my sister. Blessings on the generous, powerful women from the Center for Women War Victims in Zagreb.

I want to thank the extraordinary people at HERE Theatre in New York, who were crucial to the successful run of the play there: Randy Rollison and Barbara Busackino for their profound devotion and trust in this work; Wendy Evans Joseph for her magnificent set and great generosity; David Kelly; Heather Carson for her sexy, bold lights; Alex Avans and Kim Kefgen for their patience and perfection and for dancing the coochi snorcher dance with me night after night.

I want to thank Stephen Pevner for his great support in getting all this off the ground, and Robert Levithan for his trust. Thanks to Michele Steckler for being there again and again; Don Summa for getting the press to say the word; and Alisa Solomon, Alexis Greene, Rebecca Mead, Chris Smith, Wendy Weiner, *Ms., The Village Voice,* and *Mirabella* for talking about the piece with such love and respect.

I want to thank Gloria Steinem for her beautiful words and for being there before me, and Betty Dodson for loving vaginas and starting all this.

I want to thank Charlotte Sheedy for respecting me and fighting for me, and Marc Klein for his day-to-day work and his enormous support and patience. I want to thank Carol Bodie: her belief in me has sustained me through the lean years, and her advocacy has pushed the work past other people's fears and made it happen.

I want to thank Willa Shalit for her great faith in me, and for her talent and courage in bringing my work into the world. I want to thank David Phillips for being my ever-arriving angel, and Lauren Lloyd for the big gift of Bosnia. Thanks to Nancy Rose for her expert and kind guidance; a special thank-you to Marianne Schnall, Sally Fisher, Feminist.com, and the V-Day Committee.

I want to thank Gary Sunshine for coming at the right time.

I want to thank my extraordinary editor, Mollie Doyle, for standing up for this book in more houses than one, and for ultimately being my great partner. I want to thank Marysue Rucci for seizing the project and helping me find its way as a book. I want to thank Villard for not being afraid.

Then there are my friends-blessings: Paula Allen, for jumping; Brenda Currin for changing my karma; Diana de Vegh, whose generosity healed me; James Lecesne, because he sees me and believes; Mark Matousek for forcing me deeper; Paula Mazur for taking the big journey; Thea Stone for staying with me; Sapphire, for pushing my boundaries; Kim Rosen, who lets me breathe and die.

I want to thank great women: Michele McHugh, Debbie Schechter, Maxi Cohen, Judy Katz, Judy Corcoran, Joan Stein, Kathy Najimy, Teri Schwartz, and the Betty girls for constant love and support. I want to thank my mentors—Joanne Woodward, Shirley Knight, Lynn Austin, and Tina Turner.

I want to thank my mother, Chris; my sister, Laura; and my brother, Curtis, for finding the tangly way back to each other.

I want to acknowledge the brave, courageous women in the SWP program who keep facing the darkness over and over and riding through, particularly Maritza, Tarusa, Stacey, Ilysa, Belinda, Denise, Stephanie, Edwing, Joanne, Beverly, and Tawana.

I want to deeply acknowledge the hundreds of women who let me into their private places, who trusted me with their stories and secrets. May their stories lay the path for a free and safe world for Hannah, Katie, Molly, Adisa, Lulu, Allyson, Olivia, Sammy, Isabella, and others.

I want to thank my son, Dylan, for teaching me love, my daughter-in-law, Shiva, and my granddaughter, Coco, for birth.

Finally, I want to thank my partner, Ariel Orr Jordan, who co-conceived this piece with me, whose kindness and tenderness were a salve, were the beginning.

Many more people have become involved in *The Vagina Monologues* since the original publication of the book.

Thank you to Joy de Menil for her insightful, passionate, and careful work on this edition, and for pushing me to write more.

I want to thank George Lane for his tenderness, his advocacy, and for believing in me.

I'd like to thank Pat Mitchell for her exquisite friendship.

Since the first publication of *The Vagina Monologues*, the play opened Off-Broadway at the Westside Arts Theatre on October 3, 1999. This production gave the play its second life.

I would like to thank David Stone, the lead producer of this production, for his extraordinary vision, tenacity, faith in *The Vagina Monologues*, and for bringing it out out out into the world. I would particularly like to thank him for jumping into the V-Day movement with both feet, and for finding a way to support the movement through ticket sales.

I would like to thank Joe Mantello for his great flair, understated and beautiful direction, for getting me to take myself less seriously, and for convincing me to take my shoes off.

I want to thank Abby Epstein for her thoughtful, wise, and delicate ways of guiding women, and for being such a great support.

I want to thank Nina Essman for her belief in *The Vagina Monologues*, her incredible hard work, and for helping me find a dress.

Thank you to Eric Schnall for being such a personable, loving, smart outreach into the wider community.

I'd like to thank Bob Fennell for his grace and dignity in bringing *The Vagina Monologues* into the wider world.

I want to thank Loy Arcenas for magical vulva curtains, and for his eye for perfection and grace; Beverly Emmons for the stunning array of pinks and reds and purples, and for lighting the show in a way that made me feel both feminine and fierce.

I want to thank Barnaby Harris for dog naps, mad circles before the show, his great intensity, and his protection.

Thank you to Shael Norris Mansmann for her loving hands, labia eye shadow, for ongoing wrestling with my cowlick, and for her utter care and kindness.

I want to thank Susan Vargo for her incredible work, lifesaving back rubs, and her great heart. Thank you to Michelle Bauer for delicious maple cookies in the middle of the winter and for making me laugh.

Many other people were responsible for the big life of *The Vagina Monologues*, both by work at the theater and outside the theater. I'd like to thank Domonic

Sack, Joel Pape, Jung Griffin, Rob Conover, Arthur Lewis, Jim Semmelman, Karen Moore, Anna Hoffman, Dan Markley, Mike Skipper, The Araca Group, Amy Merlino, Patrick Carullo, Erica Daniels, Peter Askin, Terry Byrne, Eric Osburn, Russell Owen, Suzanne Abbott, Robert Fortier, Thomas M. Tyree, Jr., Marissa Yoo, Kate Sullivan, Chad Ryan Means, Charlie Chiv, Donald "Buck" Roberts, Bill Butler, David Kalodner, Tony Lipp, Josh Pollack, Gary Gersh, Larry Taube, and Sue Liebman.

Finally, I would like to thank all the actors who have generously and brilliantly performed *The Vagina Monologues*. I bless them for their great talent and their willingness and their desire to stop violence toward women.

EVE ENSLER's Obie Award–winning play, *The Vagina Monologues,* currently enjoying a sold-out run at Off-Broadway's Westside Theatre and playing in theaters all over the world, initiated V-Day, a global movement to stop violence against women. Ensler's performance in *The Vagina Monologues* will be seen on HBO in 2001. Her play *Necessary Targets* has had benefit performances on Broadway, at the National Theater in Sarajevo, and at the Kennedy Center, and will open in New York this year. Other plays include *Lemonade, The Depot, Floating Rhoda and the Glue Man, Extraordinary*

Measures, Ladies, and *Scooncat.* She is working on a new book and play, *The Good Body.* Ensler received a 1999 Guggenheim Fellowship in Playwriting. She lives in New York City with her partner, Ariel Orr Jordan.